THRIVING

IN THE

CROSSCURRENT

THRIVING

IN THE

CROSSCURRENT

**Clarity and Hope in a Time of
Cultural Sea Change**

JIM KENNEY

QUEST
BOOKS

Theosophical Publishing House
Wheaton, Illinois ★ Chennai, India

First Quest Edition 2010

Quest Books
Theosophical Publishing House
P. O. Box 270
Wheaton, IL 60187–0270

www.questbooks.net

Cover design by Dan Doolin

Cover art: Stocktrek Images/Getty and Bigstockphoto.com

Text design and typesetting by Wordstop Technologies, Chennai, India

Library of Congress Cataloging-in-Publication Data

Kenney, Jim.
Thriving in the crosscurrent: clarity and hope in a time of cultural sea change / Jim Kenney.
   p.   cm.
Includes bibliographical references and index.
ISBN 978-0-8356-0876-3
1. Social change.   2. Social evolution.   I. Title.
HM831.K467 2010
303.409'045—dc22   2009048518

Printed in the United States of America

4   3   2   1   *   10   11   12   13   14   15

This book belongs as much to my wife, Cetta, as it does to me. Her deep understanding of the nature of sea change, coupled with her insights, critiques, and patient encouragements brought it to life. I am forever grateful.

Contents

Illustrations

Acknowledgments

Do you ever sit and watch the credits roll by after a film you've enjoyed? For me, it's always astonishing to realize how many people contributed their very best in countless roles to bring the movie home. As I contemplate this project, I'm struck by the same thought. Although there is no way for me to list all those friends, advisors, critics, and acquaintances that brought something to *Thriving in the Crosscurrent*, I want at least to call up these fine folks:

Our large and close-knit families; my parents, Marylou and Jim; our very adult children (Olya, Katya, Brian, and Mary Jo); and the many lifelong friends who endured countless conversations about whether or not culture evolves, and enriched every one of those talks.

My first real teacher and lifelong colleague, Ron Miller.

My wonderful collaborator Bruce Wexler, who taught me so much about building a book.

Sharron Dorr, Richard Smoley, Will Marsh, and all the people at Quest Books for their encouragement, hard work, and editorial insight.

All my many friends, students, teachers, and fellow explorers—at Common Ground in Deerfield, Illinois, and in so many other venues—for their confidence, companionship, loving critique, and support.

My countless friends and colleagues in the global interreligious movement, some of whose organizations I list here, though many more deserve and have my deep gratitude. The International Interreligious Peace Council, the Council for a Parliament of the World's Religions, the International Interfaith Centre, the Interreligious Engagement Project, the International Association for Religious Freedom, the World Congress of Faiths,

ACKNOWLEDGMENTS

the World Conference on Religion and Peace, the United Religions Initiative, the Association for Global New Thought, and so many other groups working to bring a new vision of peace, justice, and sustainability to life and to light.

My colleagues, partners, mentors, and inspirers over the years: Saleha Abedin, Swami Agnivesh, Abdullah Ahsan, David Abram, Jay Alexander, Lydia Alpizar, Hizkias Assefa, Ron Bagby, Bud and Michelle Baldwin, Thomas Berry, Marilyn Biederer, Dolores Boot, Marcus and Mary Braybrooke, Herbert Bronstein, Eric Carlson, Swami Chidananda (Muniji), Joan Chittister, Chung Hyun-kyung, Ewert Cousins, His Holiness the Dalai Lama, Jamshid Damooei, Kathy DeFrancis, Vince DeFrancis, Ven. Dhammananda Bhikkuni, Riane Eisler, Joe Elder, Barbara Fields, Bill French, Steve Grabowski, Mark Greenberger, Lonnie Hanzon, Barbara Marx Hubbard, Gonzalo Ituarte, David and Elena Johnson, Yahya Kamalipour, Lauri Kamm, Thomas Keating, Peter Kenney, Irfan Khan, Sallie King, Paul Knitter, Marcelline Koch, Hans Küng, Mary Lamar, Todd Lorentz, Mairead Maguire, Wangari Maathai, Marcia McInerney, Bill McKibben, Ron Miller, Kamran Mofid, Rashied Omar, James Quilligan, Alan Race, Marsha Ray, Marjorie Lindsay Reed, Ahmad Sadri, Mahmoud Sadri, Ven. Samdhong Rinpoche, Don Samuel Ruiz Garcia, Kitten Sheridan, Susan Simonetti, Ann McNamara Smith, Ven. Geshe Lhundup Sopa, Charlene Spretnak, Brian Swimme, Swami Tapasananda, Wayne Teasdale, Ross and Janice Thompson, Mary Evelyn Tucker, Bill Ury, Levi Weiman-Kelman, Georgene Wilson, and so many others who should be on this list.

— Introduction —

Why This Book, Why Now?

Thriving in the Crosscurrent has been a labor of several years of research and writing. But as I reflect on the project now, it's clearer than ever that the central concept—cultural evolutionary *sea change*—rests on four intellectual pillars.

I'd like to offer a personal introduction to these structures. That is, I'd like to share my discovery of them and the intellectual excitement that drove me to write this book. As you'll learn, the experience convinced me that, despite appearances to the contrary, things are getting better rather than worse in our era; that this is one of those rare times in world history where old values and beliefs give way to new values and beliefs; that we are in the midst of what I call a *sea change*. To understand this premise, let's examine its four foundations: *interdependence, paradigm shift, cultural evolution,* and *the emerging global consensus of values.*

The first critical idea is that all existence is woven together in an interdependent web. Interdependence has been a central organizing principle for me since I first encountered the exquisite Mahayana Buddhist version of the concept in the work of my graduate advisor, Professor Isshi Yamada, and his own teacher and mentor, Dr. Hajime Nakamura.

The Buddhist teaching of interdependence has often been misunderstood as representing a complex causal system of countless elements. Actually, it lies at the heart of the famous (and equally misunderstood)

Buddhist notion of no-self. If everything exists in interdependent relationship to everything else, no thing is a "thing in itself." This seemingly puzzling idea can be grasped easily if you recognize this truth: no person, no thing, no act is an island. The Buddha is simply reminding us that no thing exists outside the context of infinite relationship to all other interdependent things. The Vietnamese Buddhist spiritual teacher and peace activist Thich Nhat Hanh puts it beautifully: "The simple fact is, we *inter-are*."[1]

When I became hooked on interdependence as a philosophical insight of tremendous explanatory power, I began to seek it out in traditions closer to home—in Western philosophy, Christianity, and Western science. It was there, of course, but surprisingly rare in philosophical and theological thought. Intriguingly, the richest yield came from the depths of Western mystical expression and the far reaches of science. Mystics like Meister Eckhart and Julian of Norwich were no strangers to the concept. Later thinkers like Jürgen Habermas and Jean Gebser plumbed its depths. And in twentieth-century science it appeared frequently in discussions of the nature of systems. From subatomics to ecology to the rediscovery of the mind-body link, holism seemed to be making its mark.

In time, this fascination took form in my graduate dissertation, "The Eye of the Triangle," a comparative study of Buddhist philosophy and twentieth-century Western physics, with an addendum on Christian theology. In it I argued that interdependence is a key factor in all three systems. I still believe that exploring the ways in which systems—including the universe itself—interdepend is the most central, productive inquiry of our time.

The second source of inspiration came from my discovery of Thomas Kuhn, the historian and philosopher of science. His controversial *The Structure of Scientific Revolutions* has long been one of the two or three most often cited books in modern scholarly literature. Kuhn's famous idea—also routinely misrepresented—is that changes in prevailing scientific theory often come about catastrophically. That is, they win acceptance only after the collapse of an earlier dominant paradigm—a set of assumptions, ways of thinking, and "things known to be true" in a particular field. Paradigm shifts always result from a swarm of anomalies, scientific results that fly in the face of well-supported expectations.

I encountered Kuhn's ideas while researching my dissertation. I confess that my first infatuation suffered from a much broader interpretation of "paradigm shift" than the philosopher would have allowed; paradigm shifts of every sort seemed to be underway in nearly every field of inquiry. I still believe that to be the case, but realize that his remarkable work bore only indirectly on my interest in broader cultural patterns outside the fields of science.

Still, Kuhn's greatest contribution to my own understanding of cultural value change was his pairing of the terms *paradigm shift* and *anomaly*. In order for an established set of values (in science, morals, or culture at large) to decline in influence, some of its principle dogmatic concepts must begin to lose their persuasive power. While Kuhn and his followers might find this statement a gross oversimplification, it is quite useful in analyzing cultural change. Without Kuhn and his anomalies, I'm not sure I would have been convinced that ours is a time of significant—interdependent—paradigm shifts.

Here's one more key thing I learned from Kuhn: belief in shifting paradigms differs sharply from belief in progress. Faith in the steady advance of progress assumes that today's guiding principles, values, and premises will remain sound tomorrow. In fact, the advance through anomalies and paradigm shifts proceeds very differently. It operates in the certainty that sooner or later today's assumptions will no longer be fully attuned to our deepening understanding of reality.

This brings us to the third foundational idea: cultures evolve to facilitate a better fit between their guiding values and the real world. It's a concept I learned to articulate fairly easily but could defend only with great difficulty.

After graduate school, I taught at the college and graduate levels in religious studies and directed an adult study center, Common Ground, cofounded with Ron Miller, a former teacher and now a close colleague. Soon my research and teaching began to reflect the realization that something more comprehensive than scientific paradigm shifts was underway. The importance of the concept of interdependence began to be cited in discipline after discipline. It began to shape the discourse in health care, education, science, social science, geopolitics, ecology, and many more fields. In an interdependent universe, after all, shouldn't systems of thought, values, and ways of seeing be as interpenetrating as physical systems were proving to be?

I came to see the growing recognition of interconnectedness as an indicator of a major cultural evolutionary shift. Some fifteen years ago, I contributed the introduction to a book on the meeting of science and religion. It contained this passage: "We live in a time of transition from mechanistic and reductionistic models of experience to models that may be characterized as holistic, or even 'organic.' The most central fact of the modern shift is the rediscovery of the interdependence of all existence. Its characteristic theme is the convergence of what had seemed impossibly disparate and unrelated dimensions of reality and modes of human experience."[2]

The freedom afforded me by my involvement in Common Ground led to the exploration of a wide range of topics—in history, philosophy, culture, religion, spirituality, psychology, and science. Each seemed increasingly inclined toward holistic approaches. And as new models developed, new insights into the nature of reality disclosed anomalies, new understandings not predicted by older ways of thinking. In health care, for example, the centuries-old separation of mind from body suddenly seemed quite inadequate.

In countless fields, the buildup of anomalies weakened the dominance of the older architecture of values. Descriptions of interdependent systems were taking shape and altering some of our most basic paradigmatic assumptions about reality. With those new understandings came the gradual emergence of newer values of every sort. Culture was evolving, and that process was something I wanted to know a great deal more about.

The fourth major insight—into an emerging global consensus of new values and commitments—developed more slowly, as a result of a fortuitous opportunity that came my way. In 1988, I became a founding trustee of the Council for a Parliament of the World's Religions. Originally the group came together to create a centennial commemoration of the first international gathering of the great religious traditions as part of Chicago's World Columbian Exposition in 1893. As it happened, the 1993 gathering of eight thousand people from all over the world turned out to be much more than a commemoration. It was a parliament in its own right, a celebration of dialogue among the world's religions and cultures. Happily, it focused most of its energy on how religious communities, singly and in interreligious collaboration, could address the most critical issues facing the world at the close of the twentieth century.

While there was a great deal of profound theological and dialogical exchange, the real action for me, as program director, lay in focusing on crises facing the planetary community and asking what could be done. We determined that the great challenges lay in three profoundly interdependent areas: peace and nonviolent conflict resolution, social-economic justice and human rights, and ecological sustainability. Our inquiries into these areas also revealed that much was already being done, with increasing effectiveness. It was my first glimpse of the emerging global consensus of values and strategies. The experience of a new wave of emerging values was confirmed and deepened when I served as global director of the parliament and helped to create the 1999 parliament in Cape Town, South Africa.

That new global consensus is exemplified by inspiring realities I have been privileged to observe firsthand. They are the major themes of this book and include:

- the centrality of peace, justice, and sustainability;

- the growth of the global interreligious movement toward pluralistic dialogue and compassionate service; and

- the new phenomenon of globalization from the bottom up—the ever-growing network of groups, nongovernmental organizations, intergovernmental agencies, and committed individuals who are striving every day to build a better world.

But none of this would be happening if humankind's dominant cultural values and assumptions were not undergoing a rare cultural evolutionary transformation—a sea change. It is a phenomenal occurrence, one that offers not only hope at a time of major global challenges but clarity at a time of increasing uncertainty and confusion.

Thriving in the Crosscurrent sets out a rich array of possibilities. While the focus is primarily on life and culture in the United States, the animating concern is global. The text touches on issues of psychology and sociology but is hardly a social scientific study as such. It has a deep interest in historical (and historic) matters but is not a history. Nor is this a spiritual or philosophical primer, though it is filled with interesting spiritual questions.

It is, I hope, a persuasive essay about one of the most important passages in the course of our human journey. You be the judge. Perhaps the greatest and most humbling stage of the entire adventure was the realization that I was far from alone. I was barely *in* the parade, much less near the front. So many others had led the way, each with her or his uniquely valuable point of view. I hope the one presented here is as helpful.

History says, Don't hope
on this side of the grave,
But then once in a lifetime
the longed for tidal wave
of justice can rise up
and hope and history rhyme.

So hope for a great sea-change
on the far side of revenge.
Believe that a farther shore
is reachable from here
Believe in miracles
and cures and healing wells.
—Seamus Heaney, *The Cure at Troy*

1

Rhyming Hope and History

Imagine an ocean moment: two waves converging in the same time and space. One is powerful but subsiding, the other just gathering momentum and presence but not yet cresting. At the moment of their meeting they are nearly equal in amplitude and influence. As they cross, who can say which is rising, which descending? In that moment only the chaos of wave interference exists.

Now imagine *modernity* as a powerful wave of cultural values that crested half a century ago and is slowly beginning to subside. At the same time, a second wave of countervailing values rises equally slowly, building until its crest begins to rival the declining energy of the older wave (see fig. 1.1 on the following page).

In Western culture the modern wave has long been dominant. Deeply rooted in classical antiquity and European history, the modern wave has profoundly shaped every culture in the world. In our own time, however, we have begun to sense the weakening of its influence and to recognize the growing strength of a challenging newer value wave.

This younger wave represents positive change. It is the wave of future possibility in the present, the advent of a cultural evolutionary transformation.

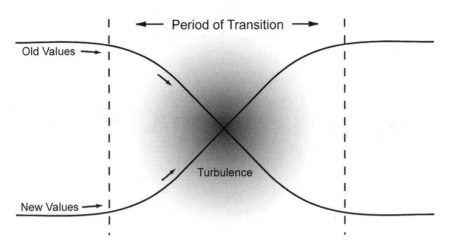

Figure 1.1 . Two Waves

Sea Change: The Good News

Not long ago, my wife and I were joined by two of our adult daughters as we rewatched a few hours of a wonderful video series. David Halberstam's *The Fifties* is an engaging but often critical portrait of the decade, based on a renowned journalist's celebrated book. Different chapters address American attitudes in the 1950s toward racism, sexuality, advertising, suburbia, war, and so on. What made watching with our daughters so amazing was the discovery that while my wife and I had lived through the period and somehow outgrown or overcome many of the more disturbing sociocultural attitudes depicted, these young women had never harbored them at all.

They alternated between hysterical laughter at some of the depictions of American women and outright horror at the stark images of American racism. Well-educated young people, they nevertheless asked again and again, "Was it really ever like that?"

I often suggest that those who are skeptical about the idea of cultural evolution should consider the differences in values that separate them from their parents or grandparents on the one hand and from their own children on the other. Attitudes toward other races, other religions, and other cultures make good starting points for such comparisons. Ideas about justice and the human relationship to the Earth offer others. Most of us will have no trouble recognizing a significant cultural shift.

As the long-dominant older wave loses amplitude and the newer one surges, we cross the threshold into an interesting time. The cultural critique—of patriarchy, the legitimacy of war, ecological exploitation and pollution, racism, injustice, religious exclusivism, and imperialism—has arguably never been more pronounced. At the same time, we've begun to explore and even embrace emerging values including non-violent conflict resolution, universal human rights, social and economic justice, ecological sustainability, and interreligious harmony.

But the passage is anything but straightforward. The interference of two culture waves unleashes both apparent chaos and emerging order. This dynamic creates the signature turbulence of a sea change: a profound alteration of cultural values toward a better fit with current realities. Sea changes are rare—in this book, I identify only four since human prehistory. They are daunting but richly creative periods, with at least three recognizable benchmarks:

- a dramatic increase in cultural complexity;

- a growing awareness of the interdependence of all with all; and

- a variety of new multiperspectival approaches to knowledge and action.

Never easy transitions, such evolutionary shifts in values produce profound inspiration and originality and, at the same time, cultural confusion and identity crisis. And, of course, the widespread emergence of new values and new ways of thinking always threatens established structures of power, thus adding a dangerous intensity to an already-volatile cultural mix.

For all that, the current sea change is very good news indeed. The idea of a sea change offers hope, and the two-wave model gives us insight into the troubling times in which we live. To find our way in a time of shifting values we need to consider the following questions:

- What are the dynamics of twenty-first-century sea change in our own lives, in American culture, and in global society?

- What is the character of an age of sea change?

- What does it mean to live in such a time of crossing?

- How do we cope and how can we contribute?

- How can we distinguish between "old-wave" patterns and those of the "new wave"?

- What are we to make of destructive phenomena that belong to neither culture wave but emerge from the turbulence of the crossing?

- What triggers such a major shift in values?

The Power of Anomalies

Sometimes I visualize a group of women on an American college campus in the mid-1960s. In my mind's eye, they've just returned from a meeting or a demonstration to advance the struggle for the rights of women. It's been a frustrating day. Most men just don't seem to get the point, and far too many women dismiss the movement as a threat to traditional gender relationships. But the members of this imaginary circle did not give up, just as the women they represent did not surrender. In time, their movement grew steadily more organized, articulate, and effective. They directed America's attention to an anomaly at its cultural heart. As we look back over the span of forty years, it's hard to comprehend fully the amazing transformation of American (and global) society and culture that the campaign for women's liberation has already accomplished.

This example shows the role of *anomaly*: telling us our models may be wrong and prompting us to challenge them. The anomaly is not the bad rule or assumption (women are incompetent), but the unexpected result (women performing well in responsible positions).

For millennia, the notion of the innate superiority of the male was rarely challenged. While women certainly knew better (and knew it eons ago), the fact that the patriarchs' assumption was terribly wrong did not become fully apparent until the modern age. The anomaly—the unexpected fact—was the increasingly apparent ability of women to excel in the very areas of life for which they had traditionally been deemed unsuited. By the late twentieth century, the buildup of anomalies could no longer be ignored.

Just consider that if all modernity's animating assumptions about the world were entirely correct:

- men would clearly be superior to women;

- war would produce peace;

- global economic and social justice would be unnecessary (and impossible);

- the concept of universal human rights would be unthinkable;

- humans could never really damage the Earth;

- one civilization would be worthier than every other;

- only one religion could be valid;

- the spiritual dimension of life would be far less significant than the material;

- no field of study would mean much to any other; and

- the pinnacle of cultural evolution would already have been attained.

In each case, our experience of the real world contradicts the expected outcome. The fact that women are demonstrably equal or superior to men in important ways is a modern anomaly. The fact that war does not, as a general rule, produce peace is another. And scarcely anyone could seriously argue that we have reached the cultural evolutionary summit.

When we begin to notice the falsity of something that was supposed to be true, we encounter the disturbing presence of anomaly and we begin to wonder. When a cultural period comes to be characterized by an astonishing buildup of readily apparent anomalies, change is all but inevitable. Welcome to the twenty-first century!

Signs of Change

The rising tide of the current sea change incorporates new understandings of the physical world, new social structures and interactions, new cultural and religious as well as intercultural and interreligious dynamics, and a revaluing of the inner dimension of human existence. Examples are easy to provide.

The brief list that follows hints at the energy and hope of countless people who are committed to trusting forward toward a better future. To be sure, many of the events and trends listed below are in their early stages; some seem to be fighting long odds. But that's the nature of a movement or a major value shift, and the following patterns are indicative of the rise of a new culture wave:

- a global movement opposing war as an instrument of state policy, coupled with the advance of nonviolent approaches to conflict resolution;

- the decline of patriarchy and the rise of new models of gender partnership, along with a dramatic upswing in women's leadership;

- a new global emphasis on social and economic justice and universal human rights;

- a resurgence of environmental awareness, new models for ecological sustainability, and unprecedented planetary commitment and activism in opposition to powerful anti-ecological values;

- a variety of serious efforts to shape multiple dialogues of civilizations as a real alternative to older-wave prophecies of a clash of civilizations;

- increasing openness to interreligious engagement, the growth of inclusivist and pluralist thinking as a counter to exclusivist and fundamentalist intolerance;

- rising spiritual hunger, a revitalized spiritual search, and deepening of spiritual practice expressed in many different forms;

- the new interspirituality, active awareness of and engagement with the spiritual paths that have shaped the world's great traditions;

- the convergence of wisdom teachers, experts, scientists, social and political visionaries, and activists to produce truly integral approaches to personal and planetary advancement; and

- a surge of interest in new ways of understanding and modeling cultural evolution.

These values form the nucleus of an emerging consensus that opposes globalization from the top down—the creeping Westernization and Americanization of the planet. The younger wave clearly represents a very different global order, a sort of globalization from the bottom up. Around the world, there is a noticeable shift from ethnocentric to world-centric values.

Each failing cultural dynamic of the older wave—sexism, racism, intolerance, fundamentalism, injustice, eco-abuse, imperialism, or materialism—manifests the essential blindness of ethnocentrism. That pathology is nurtured by the conviction that one's own group, gender, race, class, nation, species, or way of living is somehow inherently superior to every other.

So Why Doesn't It Feel Like It?

Some readers may protest that the state of the world seems to reflect very different trends. We are moving, they may argue, in an ethnocentric direction. World centrism is just a foolish dream. The global political or social or cultural reality doesn't suggest evolution. We are daily faced with everything from incivility to global violence. The realities seem to argue for devolution.

I meet this reaction all the time, and that's actually a good thing. It reminds us all that we do not yet live in the period of new-wave dominance. Ours is the time of *crossing*. The habits of thought that nurtured patriarchy, harbored racism, estranged civilizations, tolerated injustice, refined the arts of war, and presided over the rape of the planet have been challenged as never before. Their influence has sharply lessened, but their institutional and cultural infrastructures remain in place. At the same historical moment, however, a powerful array of contrasting values, hopes, and dreams is taking shape as a new cultural wave ascends to take the place of the receding older tide.

In every sea change, a moment arrives at which the influence of the declining value wave and that of the ascending newer wave are approximately equal. Our own period of crossing has, for better and for worse, appeared. Chaotic change and vanishing certainties will produce identity crises and challenges to existing power structures. Various forms of extremism will necessarily emerge to make the crossing even more turbulent. However, new understanding, values, and commitment will also enrich and enliven it. And it's essential to remember one more thing: the newer wave has momentum on its side. When you're part of the next big thing, you exude energy and confidence.

Finally, we'll take up another essential question along the way: What proportion of a society must be committed to a movement for cultural evolutionary change for the movement to be effective? The good news: it's a smaller percentage than you might think.

Yeas and Nays

If we think of a continuum between two poles—the pole of hope and the pole of fear—then we can imagine that at any specific moment each of us is situated at some place on that continuum. In times when a large number of people feel their attention being drawn more toward the pole of fear, we can talk metaphorically about a flow of social energy moving in that direction. And we can experience in ourselves how frequently the voices of fear pop up precisely at the moment when our energies are moving toward hope.
—Rabbi Michael Lerner, *The Left Hand of God*[1]

One useful way to begin to think through these issues is to identify some of the most characteristic responses to the newer ideas and values that are emerging in the crossing. How do people respond to the sea-change model itself? Over the last several years, I've been asking persons of all sorts, from every walk of life, whether they believe we're living in an age of moral growth or a time of moral decay. While the "moral decay" answer is somewhat more common, there's no shortage of vibrantly positive replies. I've come to think of the two groups of respondents as the yeasayers (moral growth) and the naysayers (moral decay). Over the last few years, I've broadened the question, but the patterns of feedback (yeas and nays) have remained fairly consistent. These days, I tend to ask for reactions to the sea-change hypothesis, the two-wave model, and the notion that ours is a time of accelerating cultural evolution, and attitudes toward some of the most important aspects of the newer wave (peace, justice, sustainability, interreligious harmony, interdisciplinary and integral knowing, etc.).

Not surprisingly, there turn out to be more ways to say yea and nay than can be taken up here, so we'll focus on the most common categories in each group.

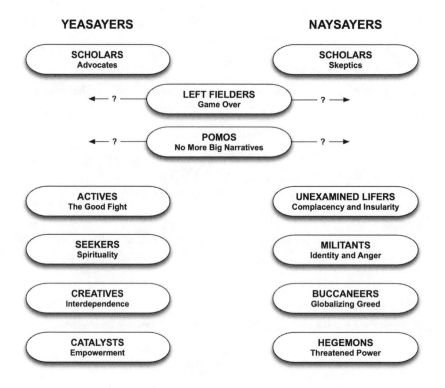

Figure 1.2. Living in a Time of Cultural Evolution?

I was born and raised in Colorado, with the Rocky Mountains as my compass and frequent destination. I live somewhere else now but return home often and am certain that no place in America has a richer distribution of cultural outlooks. I feel at home among the integral thinkers, activists, and New Agers who make their home in "the socialist republic of Boulder" and almost as much at ease with the slow-drawling ranchers and farmers who dwell on the western slope of the Rockies. Though their views of the world are very different, these two culture complexes are, for the most part, made up of people true to their values and their hearts. But they have a real dissimilarity, a cultural dissonance that goes well beyond any simplistic "blue-red" taxonomy. Their disparity has everything to do with the theme of this book. My Colorado folks—strangers, acquaintances, family, and friends—span the range of responses to the possibility that we're living in a time of particular promise and responsibility. And they fall naturally into the two major groupings (Yeas and Nays).

We'll take a closer look at the two categories. But first let's meet the Scholars, the Left Fielders, and the Pomos (Postmodernists) whose views bracket the core Yeas and Nays.

The Middle Ground

Each of the two groups calls on its own scholars to articulate its best arguments. These thinkers are deeply engaged with the question of human evolution. The sea-change hypothesis is framed by their arguments. We will engage the Advocates and Skeptics throughout the book.

Next come two groups that dominate the center: the Left Fielders and Pomos. The pairing is fascinating because individuals in either group seem equally likely to move in either direction.

Left Field: Game Over

My best friend has spent the better part of his adult life trying to make a difference in the world of work. A Colorado hard-rock miner in the high–tech world of molybdenum extraction, he has worked to integrate social justice and ecology into the corporate ethic. But Ron is just about done with it all. For him, and for the few colleagues with whom he has shared the struggle, the game is pretty much over. The bad guys have won.

Under the sway of the sophisticated naysayers I will call Buccaneers and Hegemons, corporate culture these days often seems less sensitive than ever to concerns about peace, justice, and ecological sustainability. It's hardly surprising that the far left is but a memory, while the denizens of the near left have all but abandoned the "liberal" label.

The Left Fielder is—like most yea-sayers—likely to be influenced by postmaterialist values. Nevertheless, he or she frequently reacts to the sea-change mantra with a startled "How can you possibly look around you and call *this* cultural evolution?" A more tempered response often begins with the words, "I wish I could share your optimism, but . . ." As a group, however, the Left Fielders remain receptive to the notion that cultural evolution is possible and perhaps even inevitable. They are simply unpersuaded that ours is *the* age. As the new wave swells, I believe the Left Fielders are very likely to move into the Yea column.

The next group comprises those who reject the entire concept of cultural advance on philosophical grounds.

Pomos: No More Big Narratives

Postmodernist academics like Jacques Derrida and Jean-François Lyotard have enjoyed enormous influence on the European and American academic scene for the past few decades. The postmodern thinker is fascinated by the "social construction of reality"—the notion that every purported truth reflects a unique point of view. The Pomo specialty lies in the deconstruction of *metanarratives*. Western culture is unfortunately dominated by seductive big stories that purport to explain everything you always wanted to know about anything. The list of metanarratives needing deconstruction includes monotheism, all varieties of religious scripture, Enlightenment philosophy, Western science, and the myth of democracy. Postmodern philosophy first examines and then rejects all such scenarios as the exploitative tools of power elites. The big stories have all been spun to the advantage of priests, kings, and other wielders of control.

Pomo philosophy is, in a word, relativist. It insists that every account offering meaning is told from a particular vantage point and that "truth" is therefore elusive or nonexistent. Institutions and individuals who command the social, economic, and political heights, however, always dispense the current version of truth.

In many ways, postmodernism brought with it a refreshing breeze that whisked away more than a few academic cobwebs. Its irreverent scholars played a major role in exposing the anomalous hollowness of much of modernity. From the beginning of this effort, the Pomos were in company with the Left Fielders. Postmodernism's noblest contribution was its refusal to acquiesce in the metasilencing of the voices of women, people of color, the dispossessed, and the brutalized.

Many Pomos strongly embrace social, economic, and ecological justice, but they also possess an ironically absolute certainty that there are no absolutes. In their view, talk of progressive evolution of culture and cultural values is meaningless. When it comes to cultural change, there is no "better." Still, there is hope that the Pomos' commitment to justice will draw some of them to the Yea side.

Now we turn to the visionaries and the ideologues, four on each side. Their embrace or rejection of cultural evolution is grounded primarily in their personal life experience. They may or may not be directly influenced by intellectual arguments. They are neither disillusioned nor philosophically stranded. They simply know culture is getting better, or they are certain it is not. The visionary Yeas embrace the sea-change scheme because it fits nicely with their conscious experience of evolving reality. The ideological Nays reject it because it contradicts their inflexible worldview.

Yeasayers: "Yes, Of Course!"

Yeasayers are familiar with the arguments that support their views. Informed and confident, they are relatively able to identify the decline of the older value wave. They tend to embrace postmaterialist values based on aesthetic, intellectual, moral, and spiritual goals rather than materialistic ones. Some of the more thoughtful members of this group understand the older wave anomalies as harbingers of a necessary, if painful, change. Yeasayers tend in a variety of ways to recognize and celebrate the newer wave. And as we will see, they represent a variety of points of view. In general, however, we'll find the yeasayers a largely progressive group, committed to an ascending evolutionary spiral.

Actives: The Good Fight

When this book was just a germ of an idea, I had a moving conversation with a close friend who clearly wanted to believe there might be something to the notion of sea change but just couldn't make the leap. She returned again and again to the same wistful refrain: "Do you really believe that things are changing for the better?" Ironically, Lydia is a young Latin American who has been at the forefront of the movement for global peace, justice, and ecological good sense. She and her colleagues in the struggle are some of the finest exemplars of twenty-first-century sea change. Yet, although she loved the concept, her experience made her hesitate. She tended to focus on two patterns of resistance to change—fundamentalist extremism and rampaging globalization (the desperate race to Westernize and Americanize the planet). These reactive patterns daily impede her efforts for a better world. Lydia's working assumption has been that these destructive dynamics were the real manifestations of the coming world order. As we spoke, she began to acknowledge that her efforts as an agent of dramatic change embodied the real wave of the future. Today, she's an enthusiastic sea changer and finds the model a self-renewing source of energy and hope.

The Actives include people from the left and right sides of the political aisle. They differ about the appropriate course to the future but share a deep concern for their fellow human beings, for the Earth, and for all planetary life. Actives labor particularly in the social-political-ecological arena and fill the ranks of nongovernmental organizations working for the human community and the Earth in every part of the world. Perhaps most important is the Actives' characteristic energy, which flows from their love of life and deep belief in the essential goodness of human-kind. They find confirmation and a renewed sense of community in the conversation about our unique evolutionary age.

Seekers: Spirituality

A few years ago, I presented an early version of the sea-change model to an interfaith community in the American Midwest. Responses varied, with a few moderately negative replies and a larger number of positive reactions. Among those who found the idea appealing, one subgroup stood out; they epitomized the category I call the Seekers. Their re-action was inspiringly spiritual, characterized above all by a shared confidence that the divine, or the One, suffuses the universe, providing a rich array of spiritual sustenance to those who seek it. As the name of the category suggests, yeasayers in the Seekers group tend to express strongly spiritual and philosophical attitudes toward life. While many Seekers are not overtly political, they tend to exhibit commitment to values of peace and nonviolent conflict resolution, justice, human rights, gender equity, and ecological responsibility. Seekers are inclined toward communitarian and pluralist views and are very receptive to interspiritual exchange between cultures and religions.

The category clearly includes many who would consciously identify themselves with the New Age movement—often correctly criticized for fostering a shallow brand of pluralism and a one-size-fits-all approach to the complex varieties of cultures and religions. But the group seems to encompass many others who bring a significant degree of discernment, study, and reflection to their spiritual search. On balance, the Seekers are an enthusiastic and affecting group, embodying some of the most important energies of the new wave.

CHAPTER 1

Creatives: Interdependence

The Vietnamese Buddhist teacher Thich Nhat Hanh loves to remind his students that all beings "inter-are." Interbeing, he suggests, is the essential character of all life. And if there is a single idea expressing the worldview that animates the Creatives, it's interdependence, the belief that every thought, word, and deed influences and is influenced by every other. Embodying more a lifestyle than a movement, the Creatives believe that we live in a deeply interconnected and interactive universe. They try to act accordingly. If you're convinced that you live in an interdependent cosmos, you tend naturally to be compassionate.

In their book *The Cultural Creatives,* sociologists Paul Ray and Sherry Anderson describe three principal groups in modern American culture: the Traditionalists (fifty-four million, 28 percent of the population), the Modernists (eighty-eight million, 47 percent), and the Cultural Creatives (fifty million, 25 percent). Traditionalists and Modernists are, to varying degrees invested in the values, structures, and lifestyles of the older wave. Cultural Creatives, as Ray and Anderson describe them, are strongly committed to new-wave ideals, both sociopolitical and spiritual.[2]

In a sense, the Creatives bring together some of the best qualities of the two preceding categories: the visionary commitment of the Actives and the spiritual and philosophical thirst of the Seekers. Creatives often feel estranged from the dominant culture and its emphasis on material success and power. By contrast, eager to create meaningful change in their lives and the world, they embrace compassion and engagement with programs and projects that can make a difference. That we live in a time of spiraling cultural evolution is, for the Creatives, a given.

Catalysts: Empowerment

Wayne Teasdale was a spiritual voyager and interreligious pioneer who saw the truth of evolution and reveled in cultural advance. He was a prolific author (*The Mystic Heart, A Monk in the World,* and *Catholicism in Dialogue*). Wayne died in 2004, but not before he had mapped out an intriguing interspiritual path for yeasayers inclined to interreligious and intercultural pluralism. He understood (borrowing from theologian Alan Race's familiar paradigm) that *exclusivists* insist that the rightness of their own religious way denies any meaning to other paths. *Inclusivists*, he knew, are more generous, holding that adherents of faiths other than one's own, while never in possession of the whole truth, nevertheless have enough of it to find their way to salvation. But Wayne had the greatest respect for *pluralists*, those who hold out the hope that many religious and spiritual paths might converge in the truth.

Wayne was a Catalyst. He believed in cultural evolution and carried through with a commitment to the evolutionary empowerment of people at all cultural levels. Not only pluralists were on the verge of evolutionary advance; so too were exclusivists and inclusivists. Walking through a poor neighborhood, he'd comment on a passing homeless person, "That guy is only a step away from stepping up."

Catalysts have a deep appreciation for the intrinsic value of every level of cultural evolution. Unlike many yeasayers in other categories, they appreciate the older wave and cherish it as the parent of the younger. Refusing to condemn even the extremist naysayer, the Catalyst seeks ways to intensify the evolutionary advance even of those who vehemently deny the very idea of evolution. Ken Wilber, one of the greatest thinkers of our time, an iconic Catalyst (and a close friend of Wayne), has a charming way of putting it. "No one," he says, "is smart enough to be wrong 100 percent of the time."

Above all, Catalysts grasp the dynamics of crossing. Guides for a time of turbulence and transformation, they are fully aware that ours is an age of accelerating cultural advance.

Naysayers: "It's Not Happening"

Now we turn to meet the *real* naysayers, those who tend to resist the new wave in every particular. While Pomos reject the notion of absolute truth, these groups embrace it eagerly, certain that they possess it. Like the four levels of yeasayers, the four major categories of naysayers—passive, militant, self-obsessed, and imperious—occupy successive levels of cultural sophistication. Each of the four, however, embodies a destructive response to the sea change that is now underway.

It turns out that there are more ways to say nay than yea to the notion that our time has the potential for real cultural advance. The naysayers are a diverse group, made up of people from the left, center, and right of the global spectrum. They distrust the enthusiasms of the yeasayers.

Unexamined Lifers: Insularity and Complacency

During the 2004 United States presidential campaign, Thomas Frank wrote the surprising bestseller *What's the Matter With Kansas?*[3] He argued that his home state exemplified the American heartland and the explosive social backlash underway there. Frank argued that culture (and culture shift) had replaced the economy as the linchpin issue of recent state and national elections. Successful candidates ran on culture platforms but, once elected, delivered a free-market economy and globalization/imperialism package. It was a fairly simple, if deceptive, form of the classic bait and switch: if you're alarmed about abortion, gay marriage, and evolution, we'll give you a rollback in capital gains taxes, a regime of conglomeration and monopoly, and an aggressive foreign policy.

Whatever one may think of Frank's analysis, the trade-off between social and economic issues is a reality in early twenty-first-century Middle America. The country seems rather starkly divided between those who embrace issues of social justice and have real reservations about the free-trade agenda and America's presence around the world, and those who are much more concerned about decency, traditional sexuality, and the values of hard work and don't know or care that much about the nation's economic or global choices.

Among the Unexamined Lifers we find the complacency and insularity of the unchallenged, those who cherish the older values—faith, democracy, freedom, the family—but all too often as mere phrases or symbols untempered by serious reflection. As a rule, Unexamined Lifers are essentially unaware of the buildup of modern anomalies. When confronted with evidence that the emperor has no clothes—that cherished assumptions are unfounded—they avert their eyes. They see the decline of patriarchy, for example, as an unnecessary and disorienting bother. The Lifers view intercultural and interreligious pluralism as a threat to their own culture or faith.

The unexamined life means existing in a seemingly secure but ultimately fragile state; changes in life's certainties and rhythms confuse Lifers. In fact, cultural confusion in the face of societal change is perhaps the most characteristic feature of this category. Like the Militants (see the following section), the Unexamined Lifers are often exploited by those in our last two categories, the Buccaneers and the Hegemons, the most virulent of the naysayers.

Militants: Identity and Anger

Jessica Stern is an expert on terrorism and has spoken directly with many Jewish, Christian, and Muslim militants who are willing to kill and die for the sake of their religious identity. Her *Terror in the Name of God: Why Religious Militants Kill* traces her conversations with and investigations of individuals and groups that take human life in the name of God. In one of the book's most powerful passages, she quotes a terrorist who identifies his desire for vengeance. Although the individual in question happens to be a radical ultra-Orthodox Jew, his words could as easily come from any person, religious or not, who is willing to do violence to secure personal or group identity: "Revenge . . . is stressing my positive essence, the truth of my being. . . . It is like a law of nature. . . . Revenge is the return of the individual and the nation to believe in themselves, in

27

their power and in the fact that they have a place in the sun and are no longer stepped on by everybody."[4]

The Militants are armed militia members and suicide bombers of course, but they are also the self-appointed border patrollers, gangbangers, rogue cops, and religious fanatics. They all have one thing in common: their sense of identity, self-respect, and place in the world has been threatened or undone. As a result, they have no choice but to define themselves, not in terms of their own virtues, but in terms of the vices of the hated other. And they nurture a deepening anger at that other, as the following internal monologue suggests: "I am proud that I am not a woman, a Jew, a white, a black, a Muslim, a Serb, a liberal. . . . In desperation, I find myself where I find my anger; and that anger is directed at circumstances beyond my control or at some group or groups that seem somehow responsible for my pain, my failure, or the crisis of my life. Even my refuge in religion may now take the form of a pseudoheroic allegiance to a warrior God. I turn to an all-powerful one full of righteous hate, rather than to a comforter, lawgiver, wisdom source, or wellspring of love and forgiveness."

The tamer cousins of the extremists—the vocal radicals, violence-kindling bloggers, ignorance-peddling talk-radio gurus, and hate-mongering preachers—share their contempt for the other. Militants are to be found at every point of resistance to real cultural evolutionary advance. Their worldview is simplistic but powerfully motivating. It takes shape in antipathy, in the creation of lists of enemies responsible for the cultural disempowerment and disorientation that poison their lives. The supporters of creationism and intelligent design are usually Militants and Unexamined Lifers who oppose cultural evolution.

In a time of sea change, personal identity and cultural identity are challenged. Imagine the flux that agitated Europe during the medieval to modern crossing. Every aspect of human life was affected. The change in the religious landscape alone meant that no person could any longer be entirely certain of her or his identity and place in the world and before God.

In our own age, many find the world-shrinking forces of globalization unbearably threatening to their personal identities. In his book *In the Name of Identity: Violence and the Need to Belong*, Amin Maalouf offers a simple and moving reflection: "To tell the truth, if we assert our differences so fiercely, it is precisely because we are less and less different from one another."[5]

Earlier in this chapter, I asked where fundamentalists fit into the sea-change scheme. Are reactionaries of various sorts to be understood as declining old wavers or ascending new wavers? Now we can begin to shape an answer. Religious, social, and political extremists define themselves in opposition to changing times, all the while insisting that they cherish and protect some foggily defined past. Fundamentalism and parallel forms of intolerance are neither old wave nor new wave. They are phenomena of the crossing, what I call *eddies* or *counterflows*. They are most easily observed in the lives of naysayers of the first two categories, the Unexamined Lifers and the Militants, who differ principally in their willingness to cross social and legal lines to advance their absolutist agendas.

As we'll see, the Militant response may be limited to anger or may become what interreligious scholar Ron Miller calls "supramoral fundamentalism," a willingness to cross any and all boundaries in pursuit of group-identified "justice." If cultural evolution brings in its wake broader and deeper threats to how we define ourselves (as it often does), the Militant group wants no part of it.

Buccaneers: Globalizing Greed

In 1688, Henry Morgan's buccaneers ruled Port Royal, Jamaica, with the acquiescence of the British crown. Morgan's fleet of legitimized pirate ships took fortified towns on the Spanish Main and stole a gigantic fortune for England. In the late seventeenth and early eighteenth centuries, the great navies (English, French, Spanish, and Dutch) ruled the seas, but their surrogates were often the buccaneers. Originally Caribbean pirates who preyed on Spanish and French ships and colonial settlements in the islands and along the Spanish Main, the buccaneers often sailed as privateers under British letters of marque. Issued by royal governments during times of war, these documents authorized their bearers to conduct naval actions and land assaults against "hostile powers"—in other words, to steal with the blessing of the crown.

For buccaneers then and now the pursuit was and is all about money. Then, capturing prizes from enemies allowed one to live a privileged life in the home country. Now the dynamics of globalization offer extraordinary wealth and power to the front men of the wealthier nations.

The pirates of our own age make up the category I've called Buccaneers. Like its historical predecessors the modern group has four key identifiers: materialism, amorality, greed, and global expertise. Every age, of course, has had its Buccaneers, taking advantage of the structures of power and the realities of human acquisitiveness: privateers, robber barons, speculators, dishonest bankers and developers, and multinational manipulators. In our own transitional period, materialists ride the swells of capital flow. They master global legal and economic loopholes as earlier pirates mastered the currents of the oceans. Some take advantage of the system through profiteering, accounting fraud, techno-piracy, or exploitation of the powerless. Others are subtler.

These days, globalization is a preeminent topic of discussion, but in the late seventeenth century it was already underway. The buccaneers of an earlier time understood and exploited global realities dominated by European powers. In our own crossing, we see the proliferation of free-market freebooters (another name for the buccaneers who found booty for the taking wherever they went). Globalization and the market have created vast new fields of opportunity for honest entrepreneurs and piratical parasites as well. Like the robber barons of the Gilded Age, Enron's modern buccaneers sanctified their own greed, while calling that of others into question. Today's Buccaneers—technocrats and neo-conservatives—manipulate government loopholes and authorizations to serve their own purposes. When it seems appropriate, they fund political extremism, and they manipulate the Unexamined Lifers and the Militants with extraordinary skill and massive infusions of media capital.

Intriguingly, funding challenges to mainstream evolutionary theory has served the purposes of twenty-first-century Buccaneers. Through their media outlets and political action committees (PACs), the Bucs have empowered some of the most radically antiscientific initiatives of our time. But why? What could motivate scientifically literate materialists to fund counterevolutionary initiatives?

The answer is simple enough. In fact, each dimension of the newer wave represents a potential bar to the Buccaneers' gain. Increasing concern for social justice and ecological good sense can only increase costs for the privateers and profiteers. By angering the Militants and further confounding the Lifers, however, they gain political capital. Buccaneers employ the anti-evolutionary mantra to control the Militants and Unexamined Lifers.

In turn, however, the Buccaneers are driven by the collective will of the Hegemons.

Hegemons: Threatened Power

The trial of Galileo Galilei in 1633 was a watershed in relations between the church and the natural philosophers, the new scientists. Admonished in 1616 for proposing that the Sun, rather than the Earth, was the center of the "world," Galileo was brought to trial seventeen years later, following the publication of his *Dialogue Concerning the Two Chief World Systems*. Found "vehemently suspected of heresy," Galileo was forced to renounce his arguments. *Dialogue* was banned from publication, and its author sentenced to imprisonment (later amended to house arrest). He died in 1642.

His accusers were arguably less concerned about the theological implications of his assertions than they were about the medieval power structure. If Galileo was right, then the church's long-standing endorsement of a Sun-centric universe was wrong. The repercussions, however, would be equally damaging to church and state. Galileo had to be silenced.

In the past, the Hegemons (Greek for "leader"; now suggesting tyrannical domination) have been pharaohs and priests, popes and kings, conquerors and dictators. Today, they are those who are convinced their vision, expertise, and tested opposition to "evil" entitles them to control of the global nexus.

Leo Strauss was the philosophical progenitor of the neoconservative movement that dominated the American political scene in the early twenty-first century. Strauss believed that the class of "wise men" should always employ the class of "gentlemen" (the naïve aristocrats) to control the "vulgar" class. The wise in Strauss's scheme were the Hegemons—master planners and master manipulators usually operating well behind the scenes. His gentlemen would make up the public presence of the economic and political order, presidents perhaps but never truly commanders. They would be drawn from the ranks of the Unexamined Lifers and Buccaneers. The vulgar class, made up of Lifers and Militants, would be easily mastered by the manipulation of popular fears, social controversies, and chauvinistic patriotism. Strauss's model, however, may not be so much a blueprint for the future as a guidebook to the past.

The Hegemons have the most to lose in a genuine progressive upswing. They are, as a consequence, by far the most dangerous to the transforming culture. Hegemons may be sincere in their allegiance to the structures and institutions of the older culture wave. They may not see much validity in the argument from anomalies. The center of gravity of their opposition, however, lies in their determination to preserve the modern structures of wealth, influence, prestige, and power that have served them so well.

In the twenty-first-century crossing, Actives clarify the challenges; Seekers redefine the spiritual path; Creatives nurture increasing awareness of the interdependence of the cosmos and all life; and Catalysts work to advance the cultural evolution of the many. At the same time, Militants struggle to protect their own honor; Unexamined Lifers ironically cherish a changing set of absolutes; Buccaneers seek unceasingly for new gain; and Hegemons exploit the grievances of all the naysayers to their advantage. Today, the Hegemons preside over a diminishing infrastructure of resistance to change. Their latest empire begins to fade at a time of surging energy and commitment to new values and a sweeping new vision of the possible.

There has always been a Hegemon class. In every pretransitional period it has held sway. In every transitional (sea-change) period, it has been threatened, and it has reacted with dramatic force. But the Hegemons have never managed to arrest the evolutionary process. As Giordano Bruno (burned at the stake in 1600 for teaching, among other heresies, the infinity of the universe) put it, "Time is the father of truth; its mother is our mind."

It was the best of times, it was the worst of times, it was the age of wisdom, it was the age of foolishness, it was the epoch of belief, it was the epoch of incredulity, it was the season of Light, it was the season of Darkness, it was the spring of hope, it was the winter of despair, we had everything before us, we had nothing before us, we were all going direct to Heaven, we were all going direct the other way.

—Charles Dickens, *A Tale of Two Cities*

In the distant future I see open fields for far more important researches. Psychology will be based on a new foundation, that of the necessary acquirement of each mental power and capacity by gradation.

—Charles Darwin, *On the Origin of Species*

— 2 —

Just Changing . . .
or Evolving?

The sea-change lens offers us a panoramic view of the schizo-phrenic character of rapidly changing modern life. It reveals that cultures do indeed evolve and generates powerful new insights into the whys and hows of that evolution.

Cultural evolution refers to a progressive movement of key human values toward a better fit with observed reality. Human observation of reality becomes more accurate and insightful. As a result, our conscious experience of the world grows clearer and our values tend to change accordingly. Cultural evolution is usually slow and fairly steady, but not always. Exceedingly rare periods—separated by intervals of several thousand to several hundred years—are marked by explosive growth in human understanding. Such world-shaking spans witness astonishing transformations of the value complexes that shape civilization.

These are the episodes I call sea changes. The two-wave dynamic introduced in chapter 1 becomes discernable when an important fraction of humankind arrives at a shared awareness that something is amiss. Too many of our cherished older ways of thinking about the world and humankind no longer serve their purpose. Values are out of sync with reality. When that happens, cognitive dissonance on a massive scale is triggered, producing both astonishing cultural creativity and frightening backlash. What we are experiencing today is the seemingly chaotic complexity of a genuine sea change, the next step up the cultural evolutionary ladder.

To many, the idea that human culture gradually grows wiser, more cooperative, and somehow *better* is persuasive and profoundly inspiring. These creative individuals are energized by the decline of the old and the rise of the new. For them, the *aha!* experience is a touchstone for personal and group transformation. But the concept of cultural evolution also generates a wide range of critical and even hostile responses, including the rejection of the idea that "better" means anything at all. In chapter 1, we encountered the yeasayers (who embrace the idea) and the naysayers (who reject it). We'll explore these two clusters a bit more in this chapter.

First, let's turn briefly to one of modernity's most important scientific breakthroughs, Charles Darwin's theory of biological evolution. The sea-change model is a tool for evaluating human cultural evolution, which is of course strongly influenced by biological evolution. Understanding the evolutionary character of cultural change requires a basic familiarity with the simple concept that animates the biological theory.

MR. DARWIN'S DOORWAY

Darwin did not invent the concept of evolution, but he made it a nineteenth-century cause célèbre by his clear presentation of natural selection, the "Darwinian algorithm." He began by observing that individuals vary with respect to biological characteristics. As a result, individuals in a given species possess differing biological traits, some of which may prove advantageous.

Within a given species, adaptive heritable traits (those enhancing the likelihood of survival and reproductive success) are likely to increase in frequency over successive generations. Less adaptive traits, on the other hand, tend to diminish within a given species. Nature somehow selects one phenotype (a given individual's set of observable characteristics) while discarding another.

Natural selection, in other words, simply means that certain combinations of traits are advantageous enough to the individual possessing them that the likelihood of that individual's reproductive success is enhanced. Traits that carry an adaptive advantage are more likely to be passed on and to spread throughout the species. Over time, as phenotypes grow more and more distinct, the number of species increases. This realization prompted Darwin to insist (correctly) that any two species on Earth share a common ancestor.

With the publication in 1859 of *On the Origin of Species by Means of Natural Selection, or The Preservation of Favoured Races in the Struggle for Life*, Darwin opened a doorway onto countless new understandings of the varieties of living creatures. In 1871, with *The Descent of Man and Selection in Relation to Sex*, he broadened his scope and ushered in a radically new approach to the study of humankind.

The obvious question was raised almost immediately. Did the new evolutionism relate to the development and progress of human culture as well as to biology? Through the last several decades of the nineteenth century and well into the twentieth, it seemed quite reasonable to bring Darwin's big idea to bear on human groups, societies, cultures, *and* races. Human beings are, after all, both biological and social creatures. Shouldn't it be possible to draw on Darwin's insights to illuminate our social past just as he had clarified Earth's biological past?

Soon, thinkers in a variety of disparate fields sought to incorporate the Darwinian model—as they understood it. Unfortunately, their comprehension was often less than complete. The essential question, however, had been posed: how, if at all, can an understanding of natural selection in biological evolution guide our approach to changing cultural patterns?

CHAPTER 2

A Cautionary Tale

Exploration and imperial expansion had, by the middle of the nineteenth century, opened up unimaginable reaches of wealth and influence for the European powers. At the same time, the era of empire had broadened the horizons of educated Westerners and put them in touch with an astonishing variety of peoples and cultures dramatically different from their own. The new disciplines of anthropology and sociology developed in significant measure to meet the need for analysis and, eventually, classification of these new cultures. A wealth of avant-garde inquiries arose. Why do cultures differ from one another? How do they change? What stages of development do they occupy and/or move through? The application of the Darwinian principles of natural selection to these inquiries into human social order is usually referred to as social evolutionism.

Herbert Spencer, a contemporary of Darwin, was actually the first to introduce the notion of "survival of the fittest," but he applied it to human social classes rather than to biological species. Arguing that social evolution was driven by competition, he proposed that public aid to the poor was a grave counterevolutionary error.

For the privileged and educated classes of Europe and America, the latter half of the nineteenth century was awash in confident scientism and naïve optimism. (In 1875, the head of the French Academy of Science blithely announced that, by 1925, "We shall know everything.") The spirit of Progress was in the air, as eighteenth-century Enlightenment intimations of human perfectibility found expression in countless world's fairs, utopian cults, and the gilded lifestyles of the fantastically wealthy. Predictably, the era was also characterized by an elitist individualism that fed on exploitation of less advantaged socioeconomic groups. Perhaps inevitably, the century's end saw the heavy-handed application of natural selection to pressing social issues of class and race. In time, "social Darwinism" would become shorthand for the misapplication of natural selection to human culture.

Over the next half century, sociocultural evolutionism took on a distinctly unscholarly and racialist demeanor. Its gothic course ran from classism in Victorian England, to the eugenics movement and the defense of slavery in America, to the horrors of the Nazi Holocaust. By the middle of the twentieth century, the movement was in disrepute, hopelessly tainted by prejudice and the politics of stratification. The verdict—for the moment—was in: cultures don't evolve; they just change.

Renaissance

Surprisingly, by the 1960s evolutionary thinking had reentered the social scientific conversation. Some three decades earlier, a remarkable new development had begun to take shape. A movement that would come to be known as *neoevolutionism* sought to create a fresh approach to the study of cultural evolution that would make it acceptable to the social sciences. Today, a number of creative theories of cultural advance are being explored in a variety of disciplines. Scholars now tend to take an empirical approach, identifying particular aspects of culture (technology, energy use, types of labor, social hierarchy, or recognition of human rights, to name a few) as useful standards for gauging cultural advancement. Careful to avoid deterministic assumptions, they assign important roles to probability, history, environment, encounters with other cultures, etc. For these thinkers (neoevolutionists, sociobiologists, evolutionary psychologists, memeticists, and others), to speak about cultural advance, now most often understood as a function of increasing social complexity, has once again become meaningful.

The revival has hinged on a critical point. Theories about the evolution of cultures, it turns out, need not be racialist at all. Races, in fact, seem to be convenient fictions, based largely on relatively minor physical differences. New theories suggest that, genetically, humans differ only slightly from region to region. Why then do human societies differ so dramatically and how do they change? That's still the question, but

39

theoretical approaches have changed radically. Cultural evolutionism is back; but how well do these new approaches resonate with the sea-change proposition?

Before we take up that question in chapter 3, we need to consider the rocky history of the idea of cultural evolution against the backdrop of the two-wave model. What distinguishes the failed efforts of the nineteenth century from the postmodern revival?

Two Waves, Two Ways

Darwin's ambitious imitators lived and worked in the heart of fin de siècle modernity. The older wave was in its ascendancy. Anomalies abounded and initiatives on behalf of social and economic justice, racial and gender equality, and human rights were already underway. Nevertheless, older cultural rhythms dominated, and the newer wave hadn't materialized as a countervailing set of values.

The late nineteenth-century celebration of European and American modernity was anchored in the European Enlightenment's ideal of social reform and human progress. As we'll see, the Age of Reason culminated in the last great sea change, brought on by the Renaissance and the Scientific Revolution. The ideals of the period represented significant advances over the feudalist tyranny and intellectual strictures of the medieval era. But the argument that twentieth- and twenty-first-century initiatives on behalf of peace, justice, and ecological sustainability merely extend the Enlightenment worldview is seriously mistaken.

The Enlightenment celebrated individual liberty, the preeminence of reason and science, an end to the hegemony of the church, and the possibility of improving the sociocultural order. While the movement challenged many of the moribund traditional assumptions of the medieval period, it acquiesced to many others and bequeathed them to our own time. The Enlightenment set forth many of the loftiest goals of modernity, but it also incubated some of the most troubling problems of the twentieth century, from nationalism and religious exclusivism to class, gender inequity, and systemic social injustice.

Older Wave (Modernity)	Newer Wave (Postmodernity)
Focuses on individual and group fitness, measured against the standards of the period's elites.	Reflects on the fitness of values with respect to conscious experience.
Judges a social system in terms of power, order, and wealth.	Evaluates a system in terms of its organized complexity.
Grounded in assumptions about class, race, and gender.	Aspires to egalitarian ideals grounded in fairness.
Sees cultural change as a top-down phenomenon.	Understands cultural change as a bottom-up, emergent dynamic.
Interprets human experience as a zero-sum (win-lose) game: competition drives evolution.	Recognizes the non–zero-sum (win–win/lose–lose) character of existence: interdependence and cooperation drive evolution.
Analyzes societies and cultures in terms of their parts (reductionism).	Emphasizes that societies and cultures function as complex wholes, as ecosystems.
Is strongly exclusivist in its approach to other cultures, religions, and value systems. ("If I'm right, you must be wrong.")	Takes an inclusivist or pluralist stance with respect to other cultures. ("Different 'truths' may embody different but convergent points of view.")

Figure 2.1. Views of Culture and Cultural Change

America's founders were steeped in Enlightenment virtues and values. But many were also slaveholders, and most could not countenance the notion of a woman's participation in the affairs of men. Religious tolerance was championed, but its real limits were clearly established. The Enlightenment was the manifesto of modernity. Its successes made the emerging new wave possible. But its shortcomings festered and produced the anomalies that now energize the current sea change.

The older value wave helped produce the social Darwinist approach to societal and cultural evolution. Influenced by elitist attitudes toward "inferior" races and classes, leading nineteenth- and early twentieth-century thinkers rejected the notion that cultures might somehow progress.

Cultural evolution redux, however, is a manifestation of the rising newer wave. It emerges from the current sea change. The following table sets out the distinguishing features of the two very different understandings of culture and cultural change that inform these two stages of thought about cultural evolution.

CULTURE AND THE RISING WAVE

How does the postmodern sea change generate such a different understanding of culture? What follows are six ways in which new-wave thinking can broaden and deepen our understanding of the way human cultures evolve. Encountering them now will provide you with a greater appreciation of the discussion ahead, since all six themes underpin the changes explored throughout the book.

A Different Kind of Natural Selection

Growing awareness of cultural anomalies drives cultural evolution. Standards begin to shift as more and more people realize that older ways aren't working. Here the selective process favors values that are most consistent with current conscious experience. Patriarchal institutions and behaviors, for example, necessarily begin to decline in a culture that has radically changed its understanding of women.

The Speed and Direction of Change

Cultural evolution proceeds much more rapidly than biological evolution. The speed of cultural change is a function of the fit of prevailing values with changing experience. New experiences render certain older values less relevant. Awareness of these anomalous values increases. In time, a tipping point is reached and a sea change is underway.

Biological theory maintains that no prior condition—in the individual organism, the species, or the environment—can affect the direction of a particular genetic change. Giraffes do not gradually develop longer necks in order to reach loftier forage. They don't recognize a problem and set about finding a biological solution. Neck lengthening is a by-product of an extensive series of random events. The succulent leaves growing high off the ground, however, ensure that accidentally longer necks will likely prove very adaptive and be selected for naturally. The process, though, is hit-or-miss and therefore very, very slow.

In cultural evolution, something quite different is happening. Change is cumulative and directional. It is progressive—incrementally shifting prevailing values toward a closer correspondence with changing perceptions of reality. What's more, prior conditions do indeed affect culture shift. The heightening perception of anomalies focuses attention on the increasing inadequacy of a dominant value wave. At the same time, each anomaly invites a countervailing *aha* as an emerging new wave value offers a better approach to the problem. Natural selection of a sort does operate in cultural evolution. However, it differs significantly from its biological counterpart. It's directional, driven by changing realities, and much faster.

Self-Organization and Emergence

Societies and cultures take shape from the bottom up, like insect colonies in which the queen gives no instructions whatsoever. The key here lies in understanding self-organization and emergence. Ants, markets, brains, and climates are all examples of self-organizing systems. Each is a complex, decentralized order with countless dispersed elements that somehow interact and move collectively toward higher orders of organized complexity. In other words, they evolve. But their course is not directed from the top down; it *emerges* from the bottom up. That self-organization is a critical dimension of biological evolution is increasingly apparent. The sea-change model gives emergence its due in the sphere of cultural change.

Complexity on the Increase

Complexity does not mean complication. A jumbled pile of orchestral instruments is complicated. The performance of a symphony is an example of organized complexity. Cultural evolution unfolds in part through elaboration of the roles played by individuals and multiplication of networks of contact and collaboration. Much of what develops in the process is disorganized or chaotic—complication rather than complexity. However, successfully evolving systems sometimes move rapidly to higher orders of complexity. As we'll see, that process is one of the keys to biological and cultural evolution.

Non-Zero-Sum Games

This theme is emblematic of the sea-change concept, demonstrating that our evolution tends toward cooperation and interdependence rather than endless competitions involving winners and losers. Cultural evolution favors *non-zero-sum* behaviors (cooperative win-win or lose-lose interactions) over *zero-sum* (win-lose) social patterns. Even war—which would seem to be the ultimate zero-sum game—turns out to promote a high level of nonzero cooperation within (if not between) societies. Cultural evolution inexorably leads toward more complex networks and increasing interdependence—from the first step onto the savannah to surfing the Web. In other words, being human means learning to play more non-zero-sum games. And from time to time, non-zero-sumness becomes an urgent imperative.

Convergence

The two-wave framework provides a context in which the range of cultural change theories can be understood. In other words, it helps us make sense of seemingly different explanations for what's going on.

IT CAN'T BE SO

With those themes in mind, let's now play devil's advocate and explore some of the most influential arguments against cultural evolution.

Staggering Randomness

Stephen J. Gould, the late Harvard paleontologist, was widely regarded (particularly by nonbiologists) as America's premier evolutionist. He famously argued that the process of biological evolution is essentially a "random walk" akin to the nighttime stagger of a drunk with no destination. Within easily defined limits, no particular reeling path is preferred over any other. If there is a wall on one side and a curb on the other, our drunk will inevitably end up in the gutter, despite the randomness of his meanderings. The fact that evolution by natural selection produced intelligent human life on planet Earth does not mean that it would be at all likely to happen again if the process were somehow to start over from the beginning. Those who argue that biological evolution is essentially random are also very unlikely to see any arrow evident in the change of cultures over time. Gould was dismissive of cultural evolution and urged abandonment of such a misleading term: "If we want a biological metaphor for cultural change, we should probably invoke infection rather than evolution."[1]

In this nondirectional view, cultural evolution is the result of a biased overlay of the observer's own values on the culture in question. In other words, the closer a given society's assumptions and behaviors come to resemble my ideals, the likelier I am to discern an evolutionary pattern.

CHAPTER 2

Racialism and Bad Science

Biological and cultural evolution are profoundly different processes, so different that many scholars (including Charles Darwin) have warned against the confusion that can result from modeling one on the other. Attempts to apply natural selection or other evolutionary models to human cultural change—especially when guided by political motives— have often produced embarrassing results. The term *cultural evolution* has thus long been tainted by scientific racialism. The past century and a half offers far too many examples for comfort: from American proslavery anthropology to Nazi eugenics to the controversial 1994 tome *The Bell Curve*, which argued that intelligence might be racially based.

Twentieth-century biology, anthropology, sociology, and history all tended to reject classical social evolutionism. Scientists from these disciplines most often view social evolutionary methods as undisciplined and based on unfounded suppositions.

The experience of two devastating world wars also challenged confidence in progressive cultural evolution. After all, if the world could countenance the slaughter of over fifteen million in World War I and then end far more lives (and more efficiently) in World War II, how could anyone argue that our society had evolved?

No Big Pictures

Academic postmodernism goes well beyond the caution of the new social scientists attempting to revive the exploration of cultural evolution. Declaring that there is no possible "God's-eye view" of reality and truth, postmodernism sees reality instead as socially constructed. To thinkers of this stripe, all measures of truth are local and relative. Every statement of truth—religious, scientific, anthropological, philosophical, etc.—is a "text," offered from a unique, relativistic social perspective. No text can be understood or evaluated apart from its context. As a consequence, no argument can demonstrate that any cultural point of view is better than any other or that any cultural pattern is more or less advanced than any other.

Postmodernism and its critical method, deconstruction, came into prominence after the physical and philosophical devastation wrought by World War II. It dismissed the intellectual passion for "grand narratives." The great explanatory schemes, from Christianity to Marxism to classical evolutionism, are not only worthless but are also tools in the hands of power elites. The task of deconstruction is to identify the power structure in a given text. Whether one is considering the Shakespearian stage or the stages of cultural evolution, an elitist agenda is always at work, and some "opposite thing" is being silenced.

"The center cannot hold" is sometimes cited as *the* postmodern mantra. The line is from William Butler Yeats's "The Second Coming":

> *Things fall apart; the centre cannot hold;*
> *Mere anarchy is loosed upon the world.*

The source of that anarchy is the erosion of belief and the abandonment of certainty. But there are no absolutes. Absolutely.

And it's at this point that postmodernism paints itself into a corner. "There are no absolutes, except (of course) this one." The only central truth is that there are no central truths. Which is, of course, the greatest "central truth" of all.

Moral Decay?

This objection to cultural evolution is simple: things don't *seem* to be getting better. For years now, lecturing, taking part in conferences, or just traveling throughout North America and around the world, I have been asking a particular question at every opportunity: do you believe that we're living in an age of moral growth or an age of moral decay?

In one form or another, we face this question every day, simply because we are daily confronted with at least one bit of evidence in support of one position or the other. But what's really happening? Are American culture, Western culture, and world culture all caught in some mad downward spin, or are they engaged in a progressive upward spiral? That's the real question, and it provides the essential architecture of this book.

Unsurprisingly, perhaps, the most frequent response to my query is that we are caught in a disheartening and even frightening decline. Among the negative indicators most often cited are the following:

- rising violence;

- widespread injustice;

- the erosion of familiar religious and cultural values;

- declining civility; and

- the dumbing down of popular culture.

In short, these anticultural evolutionists argue that the evidence of moral decay is obvious and irrefutable.

RESPONDEO

The great Jewish theologian Martin Buber is often associated with an insightful Latin phrase, *Respondeo etsi mutabor*. It means simply, "I will respond, even though I may be changed." And so I respond here in brief to the plausible nays—though this book will unfold as a much more comprehensive response.

The very best of the nays, it seems, touch four critical points: randomness, racialism, deconstructionism, and despair. Each represents an attempt to contravene our confidence that something is indeed underway. But each is based on a false assumption about reality and/or our knowledge of it. Here, I'll briefly challenge each one. In the chapters that follow, I hope to explode the myths and misconceptions on which they're based.

A Clear Direction

The argument that evolution is nondirectional is perhaps the most important and, potentially, the most damaging of the plausible counterarguments. If no evolutionary direction exists, biological or cultural, the increase in complex forms is accidental, and the appearance of consciousness and civilization is mere happenstance. As we'll see, however, Gould and others who share his fealty to randomness miss the point. Cumulative change is strikingly apparent if we know where and how to look. Slavery was identified as an anomalous evil, and it passed away. Gender and racial inequity is fading. And the notion that the Earth is not fragile no longer makes sense. These changes are not random value shifts. Each is progressive. Growing awareness of anomaly drives each one.

Racialism on the Way Out

Actually, racialism is fading fast. Recent developments on the American political scene strongly suggest that our youngest generation is postracial. Racism remains on the scene but is increasingly socially rejected. We can easily imagine a postracial social atmosphere in the twenty-first century. Something is stirring.

Return of the Big Pictures

Academic postmodernism has enjoyed—and exhausted—its heyday. The denial of meaning and the reduction of every statement to a text that must be deconstructed to discover its hidden power-elite agenda . . .

that's all winding down. As the social sciences breathe a collective sigh of relief, it's once again possible to suggest that key narratives ("big pictures") like sea change do indeed exist and that scholars can and should attend to them.

A Time of Moral Growth

Are we living in an age of moral growth or moral decline? The simple answer lies in thoughtful observation. How do we assess the decline and disappearance of the legitimacy of slavery, of the subordination of women, of the destructive exploitation of the Earth, and even of the legitimacy of war? Change is in the air. The notion that ours is in fact an age of moral growth rather than moral decay is suddenly rather plausible.

The next chapter introduces the four essential forces of cultural evolution. Four persuasive voices lead the way.

The world remains in many ways a horribly immoral place by almost anyone's standard. Still, the standards we apply now are much tougher than the standards of old. . . . It is good that we thus agitate for further progress, and all signs are that this agitation goes with the flow of history. Still, it is hard, after pondering the full sweep of history, to resist the conclusion that—in some important ways, at least—the world now stands at its moral zenith to date.
—Robert Wright, *NonZero: The Logic of Human Destiny*

Man is not a static centre of the World, as has so long been thought: he is the axis and the "arrow" of Evolution, which is something much finer.
—Pierre Teilhard de Chardin, *The Phenomenon of Man*

3

Four Strong Winds

Cultural evolution doesn't simply happen. Just as four forces—gravity, electromagnetism, and the strong and weak nuclear forces—shape the physical universe, so four dynamics drive the evolution of culture. Just as strong currents and prevailing winds affect the play of the great oceans, the sea-change model identifies four convergent dynamics that influence every major cultural evolutionary transformation:

1. *complexity*: the evolution of consciousness;

2. *chaos to order*: how open systems advance;

3. *creativity*: bottom-up, self-organizing, emergent forms; and

4. *cooperation*: interdependence as evolutionary touchstone.

By understanding these dynamics, we can better understand why the world is changing for the better rather than for the worse. When we recognize that distinct drives underlie cultural evolution, we begin to discern the pattern behind the apparent chaos of a sea change. Despite the unpredictability of surface events, an evolutionary arrow starts to become apparent when we comprehend these four dynamic forces.

CHAPTER 3

Complexity

Human culture grows steadily more complex and, in the process, more evolved. In the context of cultural evolution, increasing complexity means simply that things become more intricate. More complex forms (values, societal roles, behaviors) interact in more complex ways with other complex forms. The system moves to the next level.

Imagine a simple village evolving into a town. As the process unfolds, more people play more complex roles. The clerk takes on the responsibilities of the postmaster and now cooperates with the bailiff, who has also become the sheriff. The doctor interacts in a new way with the apothecary, and together they shape the new office of the coroner. The functions of storekeeper and bookkeeper become more synergistic, and . . . well, you get the picture. Cultural evolution urges each participant's role in the direction of more multifaceted engagement with others. An evolutionary course of this sort will generate significant changes in basic value patterns (for example, with respect to gender roles, notions of justice, and patterns of cooperation). A dramatic increase in organized cultural complexity is one of the first discernable signs of a sea change.

Chaos to Order

In open systems (like organisms, ecosystems, brains, cities, and societies), a relatively sudden movement from apparent chaos to emerging order is possible and even likely. An open system is one that retains its essential identity while continually interacting with its environment through the exchange of energy, information, waste, etc. Input, throughput, output, and feedback mechanisms are all essential features of an open system. Still, even through apparently chaotic periods the open system retains its coherence.

Evolving cultures are open systems, vulnerable to chaotic perturbations that can lead to dramatic increases or decreases in organized complexity. The possibility of dramatic evolutionary shift in open systems affords yet another way of thinking about the process of sea change.

Every major cultural evolutionary transition must be attended by a period of transitional turbulence. During an earlier sea change, the Axial crossing, in which the major modern religious and philosophical traditions had their roots, perturbations of the great imperial orders gave rise to countless new cultic patterns. Each new religious community was capable of reaching the critical point at which it would either move to a higher order of creative complexity or regress to a simpler order and perish in the descent. Overall, the Axial period yielded a rich array of new and enduring forms of spiritual inquiry.

Creativity

Evolution occurs bottom–up, through the astonishing process of *emergence.* The persistent myth of the ant queen dispensing orders from above conceals the far more astonishing phenomenon of ant colonies organizing themselves through the combination of dogged persistence and natural chemical signaling. This blind self-organization reveals the mystery of novelty. The development of insect colonies, cities, computer programs, epidemics, and the rapid spread of ideas whose "time" has come provides insight into the surprising creativity we observe in a wide range of complex phenomena.

It seems that such creativity proceeds not downward from some overarching (or "intelligent-designing") system but upward, from the collective behaviors of relatively "stupid" networks. As we learn that evolution—and, particularly, cultural evolution—creates itself through self-organization, we should pause for reflection. That religious anti-evolutionists stand in awe of complex, creative emergent systems and imagine that only the hand of God could have wrought such things is actually quite understandable.

In the rising wave of the twenty-first-century sea change, self-organization drives the formation of surprising new cultural dynamics. How do new concerns and causes arise? Clearly, they are not always orchestrated from above. It turns out that self-organization is to our age what imperial fiat was to the late Axial. While many vital structures are in fact initially designed from the top down (consider the World Wide Web), the evolutionary processes that shape their content and behaviors are increasingly likely to emerge from the bottom up.

Cooperation

Human social evolution reveals increasing interdependence. When the first bands joined together to hunt mammoth, deer, or even rabbits, they knew they functioned more effectively as groups than as individuals. Cooperation demanded information exchange. Circling and driving game was a rather complex operation; but it worked. That success was only one of many signposts across the millennia of cultural advance.

A steadily ascending level of interactive cooperation is evident. We can trace it in Neanderthal care for wounded members of the group. It is evident in the archaeological record of complex hunting and game-sharing behaviors among fully modern humans as early as forty to one hundred thousand years ago. Even in the warlike behaviors of more advanced humans, the interdependent inclination is clear. While war itself is anything but cooperative, preparation for and participation in combat is precisely that.

In fact, the steady advance of human societies toward increasing levels of complex cooperation may be the most powerful evidence of cultural evolution. The modern period, perhaps more than any other, exemplified cooperative interaction—in exploration, science, art, and even religion—although that cooperation was often intragroup and accompanied by hostility toward outsiders.

At the threshold of the twenty-first-century culture shift, we are increasingly aware that interdependence is crucial. We must approach not only our problems, but also their solutions with a thorough grasp of synergy.

THE CYCLE

Figure 3.1 provides a visual context for the four dynamics. The circle represents a single sea-change cycle. Beginning at the six o'clock position, the left hemisphere maps the advance of a given sea change, identifying the four dynamics that drive it. The process culminates in a new order of consciousness and culture—the ascendancy of a newer dominant value wave. The right hemisphere begins (at the twelve o'clock position) with the set of cultural values brought to preeminence by the preceding sea change. It then traces the crystallization and decline of the dominant wave, the rise of the newer wave, the failing older wave (anomalies) and the emerging newer one (*ahas*). Finally, we arrive at the beginning point of the cycle. Note the critical position of the eddies—vortices of turbulent resistance to change.

The two hemispheres reflect vital features of the sea-change cycle. The four dynamics on the left not only drive the rising wave but also disclose the eventual inadequacy of the older value system. Our discussion thus far has emphasized the implications of complexity, coherence, creativity, and cooperation for a better understanding of reality and a concomitant refinement of values. However, that process clearly has as much to do with the decline of the former wave as with the rise of the newer. The two waves simply present different views of a single evolutionary cycle. They are simultaneous and synergetic. Be aware as well that this two-dimensional graphic obscures the third dimension of a sea-change cycle. Each revolution climbs to a higher level of organized complexity and awareness of interdependence. The circle actually represents a slice of the ascending spiral.

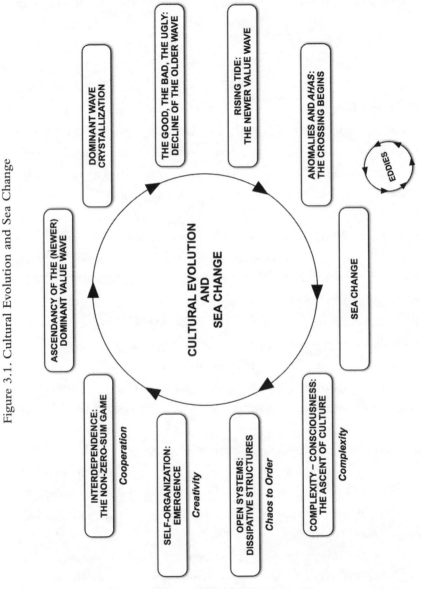

Figure 3.1. Cultural Evolution and Sea Change

FOUR VOICES

Four remarkable thinkers—Teilhard de Chardin, Ilya Prigogine, Stuart Kauffman, and Robert Wright—provide insight into the dynamics we've discussed. In the encounter with each individual's ideas, we can better understand how a given dynamic urges human values toward reality and how it warns of the danger inherent in the eddies of cultural habituation and resistance to change.

Consciousness Rising: The Complexity Dynamic

According to the controversial Jesuit scientist-philosopher Pierre Teilhard de Chardin (1881–1955), the *noosphere* is the planet's invisible envelope of collective human consciousness. The idea of the noosphere (from the Greek word for "mind") bridges the spiritual and scientific realms to create a model of collective human potential, the climax of complexity. It may sound like science fiction, but the theory was a serious scholarly attempt to bring science to bear on the ongoing process of human evolution. Teilhard was convinced that biological evolution must bring cultural and spiritual advance in its wake. The key lay in the relationship between complexity and consciousness.

He sought to demonstrate that evolution moves steadily in the direction of increasing complexity and that with growing complexity must inevitably come life and consciousness. "Complexity-consciousness" became one of the most familiar phrases in his lexicon. "Man alone constitutes the last-born, the freshest, the most complicated, the most subtle of all the successive layers of life."[1]

Teilhard's evolutionary ideas were strongly influenced by the Earth's sphericity. In the early stages of hominid evolution, especially after the appearance of *Homo erectus*, dispersal dominated as groups spread farther and farther apart from one another. As populations grew, however, convergence took over, bands moved into denser concentrations, and the hominid capacity for reflection became more refined. Eventually, as early *Homo sapiens* (the genus that includes Neanderthals and fully modern humans) emerged, larger groups came together. The spherical Earth drew humankind into reflective life, and the noosphere began to emerge. (What might have happened on an endless flat plain?)

In the twentieth century, Teilhard thought, humankind was just beginning to experience the first glimpses of the unity that was in the offing.

> The human person is the sum total of 15 billion years of unbroken evolution now thinking about itself.
> ...The spherical geometry of the earth and psychical curvature of the mind (harmonize) to counterbalance the individual and collective forces of dispersion in the world and to impose unification.[2]

The acceleration of complexity-consciousness—and of cultural evolution—is the result of *compression,* Teilhard's term for the limits imposed on human dispersal by the physical shape of the planet and the tendency of mind to seek out mind (psychical curvature).

Convergence, in other words, yielded increasing complexity, which led to the intensification of life and consciousness.

Open Systems and Dissipative Structures: The Chaos to Order Dynamic

The explosion of popular interest in chaos theory began with the 1988 publication of *Chaos: Making a New Science,* by James Gleick. While the author did not attempt to explore the details of that new science, his sketches of personalities and events drew attention to the work of Ilya Prigogine.

Born in Moscow in 1917 and raised in Belgium, Prigogine won the 1977 Nobel Prize for Chemistry for his work on dissipative structures—dynamic systems engaged in a constant exchange of energy and waste with their environments. These open systems included everything from organelles to empires, from traffic patterns to stock-market trends, and from termite mounds to cardiovascular systems. To fully appreciate Prigogine's breakthrough, however, we have to travel back in time.

The nineteenth century's prevailing scientific focus shifted from dynamics (the motion of bodies under the influence of forces) to thermodynamics (relationship between heat and other forms of energy). The second law of thermodynamics is what's relevant to our discussion: the entropy of the universe tends to a maximum.

Entropy refers to the steadily increasing unavailability of a system's thermal energy for mechanical work. The universe seemed to tend irreversibly toward an infinite broth of randomness and absolute cold. Energy and organization would inevitably be lost. Think how a cup of coffee cools or how a glass of ice melts and you'll understand how systems move toward entropy. Nature will neither reform the ice cubes nor reheat the coffee. The entropic process is irreversible. To the new generation of thermodynamicists, time's arrow leads to randomness and heat death, to perfect equilibrium.

Prigogine had a different idea. Open systems, he declared, could dissipate entropy by moving steadily toward higher and higher levels of complexity. In chaotic situations, such systems can "choose" between two alternate paths. One (usually fatal) reverts to a previous evolutionary level of lesser complexity. The other leaps to a higher order of organized complexity, an evolutionary advance.

Take a moment to imagine the "bifurcation point" that Prigogine describes. Two roads diverge: the one leading to a regressive return to an earlier organizational pattern (and death), the other toward a leap into increased complexity (and evolution). In cultural evolutionary terms, the former is a movement toward devolution and the latter is a progressive reaction to naturally occurring cultural stress.

In the nineteenth century, the second law gave rise to a cynical attitude toward universal advance. After all, if the cosmos is moving relentlessly toward a state of totally useless energy—entropy—why should we antici-pate an evolutionary outcome? This was the Darwinian conundrum. How was science to account for the apparent incompatibility of evolution and entropy? How does life wind itself up as the universe is winding down?

We find a hint in a final insight from Prigogine (who died in 2003). He argued that the more complex an open system, the greater the com-plexity of the next level it can attain. Every such transformation increases the system's complexity, thus increasing its instability and its openness to subsequent evolutionary leaps. Life, in fact, may devour entropy.

Ilya Prigogine studied termites. Of course he also studied traffic pat-terns, brains, atomic clocks, and just about everything else, but he seems to have had a special affinity for termites. The worlds of termites, bees, and ants have no real queens, just hyperactive egg layers. Unlike the world of the film *Antz*, the real ant world has no strutting generals, and the workers are certainly neither enslaved nor particularly disciplined. In fact, each insect is only as intelligent as a very tiny brain and nervous system allow. An ant is essentially stupid. No top-down instructions guide its wanderings. No royal plan is at work, only complex, seemingly random interactions. Yet somehow, out of it all, new patterns of a higher order regularly unfold.

Self-Organizing Emergence: The Creativity Dynamic

A self-organizing system is one in which internal organization increases over time without any outside direction or control. Such a system is *open*, that is, closely interconnected with its environment through strong energy flows (sunlight, heat, critical chemicals, nutrients, etc.). An open, self-organizing network finds itself in a state far from equilibrium—changing, active, even turbulent. (Think of a cold cup of coffee as just the opposite: a system in a near-equilibrium state, very unlikely to evolve.) An open system is vulnerable to chaotic turbulence and, therefore, may be able to jump to a higher level of complexity. It is quite likely to evolve, and almost as likely to devolve and perish.

We naturally tend to assume that things, left to themselves, become disorganized and messier. Imagine what it would mean if the opposite were true. What if complex systems tended, on their own, to become more complex rather than simply more complicated? Consider this analogy: a tangled pile of orchestral instruments in a hallway is complicated; a symphony, well performed, is complex.

The most intriguing feature of the self-organizing system is that it may over time yield up very stable patterns. Self-organization is at work when single cells give rise to complex multicellular organisms or when insect colonies create elaborate structures and coordinated patterns of behavior. It may well underlie much of the brain's ability to coordinate disparate sensory experiences and memories into completely novel insights, imaginings, or new value complexes.

Herein lies the mystery of creativity. The rise of novelty from the activity of self-organizing systems is now fairly well understood, especially in biology. And when we turn our attention to culture, it seems far less surprising that unexpected novelties emerge and that they often meet the needs of a developing system, well, perfectly. Can self-organization explain the sudden emergence of a creative insight or the synchronistic convergence of several different ideas? The answer is yes. In fact, many researchers regard creativity as a product of self-organizing systems whose outcomes confound ordinary reasoning. More simply put, self-organizing emergence seems to be the key to the creativity dynamic.

The surprising thing is that the entire process arises from apparently dissimilar and only haphazardly interacting flows of information and influence, like the pheromone trails that "organize" millions of ants. In the chaotic regime of the self-organizing system, insignificant alterations of basic structure can yield sweeping changes in outcome. And therein lies another key to cultural evolution.

No one understands it all better than Stuart Kauffman, one of the Santa Fe Institute's seminal figures. The institute is dedicated to multidisciplinary inquiry into complex adaptive systems (like ants, cities, hearts, markets, software, brains, and cultures). A pioneer of chaos/complexity theory, Kauffman is one of the leading cartographers of emergence; self-organization is his animating theme. His notion that such systems will often (or always) move into the "adjacent possible"—the next more complex systemic array—animates much of the current conversation about emergence. Kauffman argues that biospheres keep trying to move into the adjacent possible sphere, the next level of possible complexity. But does that apply to cultural evolution? Kauffman thinks so.

Ask Stuart Kauffman about cultural evolution and he might well observe that we are caught in the flux of two evolutionary systems. The first, of course, is biological/environmental. After all, we inhabit a biosphere that evolves constantly, which is now under internal pressure from ourselves. On the other hand, we have created a *humanosphere* that is itself unceasingly evolving, and at a much more rapid rate than the biosphere.

Simply put, self-organizing systems tend toward higher levels of internal complexity. That means that they evolve. Clearly, complexity and evolution are dynamic twins, and self-organization is at the very least a key sibling.

How then do we begin to grasp cultural evolution and to shape our planetary culture appropriately, avoiding the eddies that attend the transition? For Stuart Kauffman, that has become the essential question. In *Reinventing the Sacred*, he phrases the challenge starkly: "We lack a global ethic. We must construct one to prepare for the global civilization that is upon us, hopefully persistently diverse and forever evolving, forever inventing, and partially guide the form it will take. I say 'partially' because we cannot know all that will happen, including the consequences of our own action. Here, too, we live our lives forward, with courage and faith."[3]

The mystery prevails, but if cultures evolve—through the intensification of complexity and the proliferation of open, self-organizing systems—how do they move? Is there a preferred direction of evolutionary advance? Is there an arrow of evolutionary advance?

The Non-Zero-Sum Game: The Cooperation Dynamic

If cultures really do evolve, what can we say about the direction they will most likely take? Robert Wright has a provocative answer.

Modern game theory (which now influences countless fields) distinguishes between *zero-sum* games, in which one party wins and the other loses, and *non-zero-sum* games, in which all players win or lose together. Examples of zero-sum games range from soccer to baseball to chess. Non-zero games include the group hunt, barn raising, information exchange, collaborative problem solving, and partnerships of countless sorts.

Wright, in his acclaimed best seller *NonZero: The Logic of Human Destiny*, argues that "both organic and human history involve the playing of ever-more-numerous, ever-larger, and ever-more-elaborate non-zero-sum games."[4] The result is increasing biological and cultural complexity and cooperation—in short, biological and cultural evolution.

Humankind moves in a particular direction: toward increasing cultural complexity, toward civilization. Biological evolution, through natural selection, provides the foundation for cultural evolution.

Wright counters the view held by many biologists that the emergence of intelligent life is random happenstance. He insists that if the whole story of the hominids were to start over, the course of human sociocultural evolution would more or less repeat itself: moving steadily in the direction of greater cooperation. The human advance from prehistory depended on the increasing frequency of non-zero-sum games. The same pattern, he argues, can be observed in biological evolution itself. We can trace the development of non-zero-sumness "from the primordial ooze to the World Wide Web."

He takes us through a wide range of examples of cooperation: the hunt, commerce, exploitation of fire and seeds, and even war. Across the spectrum, the basic pattern is the same. New situations suggest cooperation, which yields clear benefits: increasing complexity generating greater awareness of and exploitation of interdependence.

Technology plays a critical role in the process: "New technologies arise that permit or encourage new, richer forms of non-zero-sum interaction. Then . . . social structures evolve that realize this rich potential—that convert non-zero-sums into positive sums. Thus does social complexity grow in scope and depth."[5]

Wright understands that many biologists strongly resist the idea of a goal of any sort in the evolutionary process. Like Teilhard, however, he links intelligence to increasing complexity and also suggests that the process gains tremendous energy from the convergence of human population groups. The likelihood of the processes of convergence, increasing complexity, and intelligent cooperation need not suggest a teleological cosmos or an intelligent designer.

NonZero suggests that history's arrow points clearly in the direction of increasingly cooperative social interaction. The human species tends to organize in bands, and bands learn to cooperate. Those that don't, perish. Wright notes that the dynamic of nonzero interdependence steadily grows in influence over the course of hominid and human evolution. We band together almost unbidden, but then we learn to cooperate. Perhaps it's the rabbit hunt or deer hunt that ignites the spark, but in time our survival-centered bands become cooperative tribes.

Finally, Wright reminds us that complacency is not an option: "War and other forms of mass slaughter, other manifestations of massive hatred, could be ended—or, on the other hand, they could set new records for death and destruction; they could even, conceivably, end us. And the outcome may hinge on the further spread of knowledge—not just empirical knowledge, but moral knowledge."[6]

THREE BENCHMARKS

In 1948 Eleanor Roosevelt, the widow of President Franklin Roosevelt, helped create the new United Nations. As chairwoman of the fledgling UN Commission on Human Rights, she was charged with forging a document that would change the course of world history. Had the world's most influential thinkers been asked fifty years earlier to give their opinion on the question of universal human rights, their collective answer would have been a resounding No! Human cultures were too disparate to share any universal idea of what things *must be done* for all people and what things *must never be done* to any person. The postwar realization of the horrors of the Holocaust had changed all that. Now, Eleanor Roosevelt and her colleagues from around the world knew that universal rights must exist and that someone must begin to enumerate them. Over half a century later, the Universal Declaration of Human Rights stands as one of the most important and influential accomplishments of the modern period, and a major influence in the current sea change.

All of which brings up the question, is the rise of universal human rights an example of genuine cultural evolution?

This question opens up a conversation about values, how they change, and how that change affects culture. My purpose here is not to predict, but rather to offer an assessment of the fact that our moment in time seems to be undergoing a largely beneficial cultural evolutionary surge. The problem, of course, arises when we attempt to identify beneficial emergent values. Do apparent changes for the better in values, choices, and behaviors indicate that real cultural growth has taken place, or are such things merely fortuitous? Moreover, who's to say if a particular cultural change is positive or negative?

That's why we need some benchmarks. In a time of real cultural progress, we will encounter a wide range of evolutionary claims. How can we sort through them and separate the authentic from the spurious? I suggest that we employ three simple standards as criteria for real evolutionary advance. It may be useful to think of the benchmarks as portable tools to test for the underlying activity of the four forces.

Taken together, the benchmarks indicate whether a given shift grows out of the action of the four forces. What we're testing for, in essence, are emergent values, understandings, and behaviors that constructively address the anomalies that agitate our age. Each authentic evolutionary value should generate an increase in three measures: complexity, awareness of interdependence, and integral knowing.

Of the four forces, two lend themselves easily to the assessment of particular sociocultural changes. Open systems seem to favor the dramatic evolutionary leaps described in the sea-change model, and they tend to favor self-organizing processes. In the short run, however, open systems and self-organization may be difficult or impossible to detect in a given cultural change. One can much more easily discover whether a particular shift has produced an increase in complexity and/or broadened cultural attention to interdependence. Our first two benchmarks, therefore, identify higher orders of complexity and greater awareness of interdependence. Simple enough.

The third benchmark may be the most broadly useful. Based on the thought of philosopher Ken Wilber, the final benchmark asks whether a given cultural variation contributes to the integration of the most important modes of human knowing. Let's take a brief look at each of these benchmark criteria.

Complexity

Cultural evolution proceeds by movement from lesser to greater degrees of organized complexity. Self-organizing systems tend to higher and higher orders of complexity and, therefore, creativity. Greater organized complexity in turn heightens the instability and, therefore, the flexibility of an evolving system—a definite adaptive advantage. More simply put, the more complex the cultural pattern, the better it can damp out the fluctuations that might destroy a less complex network.

When a system becomes more complex but less orderly, we sometimes speak of disorganized complexity. Most would refer to this state of affairs as mere complication. For example, consider that jumble of musical instruments of every sort thrown into a heap. The situation is complicated and not evolutionary. But the first notes of a new symphony, performed on those same instruments, celebrate cultural evolution.

Eleanor Roosevelt certainly envisioned a more complex global society, one in which more people understood and observed a much more detailed set of obligations to far greater numbers of their fellow human beings. The postpatriarchal social order exhibits a far more complex character than its predecessor. What's more, heightened complexity is clearly creative, giving rise to a wide range of social reconfigurations that enrich global culture.

Awareness of Interdependence

As cultures evolve, they gradually become more aware of the interdependence of the spiritual, cultural, physical, and sociological dimensions of their existence. This growth of insight has attended every past sea change. Nevertheless, in our own time we retain a tendency to focus on the separateness of things rather than on their real intertwining. That's one of the most enduring legacies of modernity. The current sea change, however, is shaped by the greatest awareness ever of deep-rooted interconnectedness. We're discovering that all living and nonliving things form intricate relationships and give rise to complex ecosystems.

To determine whether a given cultural change is really part of the sea change, we must assess both whether or not it has augmented creative complexity and whether or not it has generated broader awareness of the interdependence of various systems. Consider the sweeping realization in the late 1970s and early 1980s of the long-denied mind-body connection. For most Americans, the first encounter with the word "holistic" came in the context of an emerging discussion of health care and health styles. At almost the same time, the ecological movement was coming into its own. Two different expressions of the new wavelength were maturing in the same decade. Each brought a more complex model into cultural awareness, and each drew attention to the interdependence of authentic existence. Both expressed the sea change.

Four Quadrants: The Integral Approach to Knowing

Now, we turn briefly to the thought of Ken Wilber. The great American philosopher describes four essential realms of human knowledge and endeavor. As the figure indicates, the four are divided into two concerned with the individual (the interior and exterior dimensions) and two that address the collective (again, in its interior and exterior dimensions).

As cultures develop, their approach to knowledge becomes more and more integral as the different modes of understanding begin to be seen by more and more cultural pioneers as complementary windows through which existence and experience can be viewed and understood. Culture moves steadily (and, in a sea change, dramatically) in the direction of greater parity among the ways of knowing.

Chapter 4 introduces three earlier sea changes. In each case, look for the four forces and try your skills at applying the three benchmarks, the criteria by which we can begin to recognize "the real thing."

Interior: Individual **SELF** "I" language Art/Aesthetics, Psychology, Philosophy, Spirituality	Exterior: Individual **SCIENCE** "It" language Physics, Cosmology, Chemistry, Biology, etc.
Interior: Collective **CULTURE** "We" language Literature, Philosophy, Religion, Morals	Exterior: Collective **SOCIAL SCIENCE** "They" language Sociology, Economics, Anthropology, etc.

Figure 3.2. Four Quadrants of Knowing

Human history's most important event since the last Ice Age was the first rise of agriculture in Southwest Asia's Fertile Crescent. The origin of agriculture triggered a long train of economic, political, and technological developments, which began there and spread outward.

—Jared Diamond, "Location, Location, Location:
The First Farmers"

An axis of world history, if such a thing exists, would have to be discovered empirically, as a fact capable of being accepted as such by all men, Christians included. . . . It would seem that this axis of history is to be found in the period around 500 B.C., in the spiritual process that occurred between 800 and 200 B.C. It is here that we meet with the most deepcut dividing line in history. Man, as we know him today, came into being. For short we may style this the 'Axial Period.'

—Karl Jaspers, *The Origin and Goal of History*

— 4 —

Three Crossings

T he modern sea change was not the first. At least three other monumental cultural tidal waves occurred before our own. Each was preceded by the buildup of anomalies. Each in its turn produced eddies of resistance. And each in time prevailed.

Every sea change sets the stage for the next. Each incorporates imperfections inherent in its worldview and contradictions hidden among its core values. Together these catalyze the system failures that bring about the next cataclysmic shift. Nevertheless, each complete passage marks a dramatic cultural evolution.

We now move back in time to consider three singular human cultural crossings. Taken together, they yield insights into our own transit and make the sea-change hypothesis more concrete and plausible. Each exhibits the essential elements of a major cultural evolutionary leap: epochal shifts in understanding and the characteristic signs of culture-wave turbulence. In each account, we'll note the significance of anomalies and eddies—the dynamics of change and resistance. And each illustrates the eventual attainment of higher levels of creative complexity, awareness of interdependence, and integral understanding, for every sea change produces a better fit between culture and experienced reality.

CHAPTER 4

THE RISE OF THE FARMERS: THE FIRST SEA CHANGE

Fourteen thousand years ago a band of some thirty ice-age hunter-gatherers makes its way along the boggy terrace at the edge of the glacier. They cannot know that the ice wall towering above them—at times by more than a mile—is slowly receding. In another four thousand years it will have withdrawn far to the north, and a new age will dawn for Earth's tiny and scattered human race. Ahead of the group a meltwater channel, once only a trickle, now thunders toward the sea. Ocean waters rise steadily around the Earth as the blue glacial masses thaw. The Bering land bridge, the pathway from the Old World to the New, slowly narrows and soon will vanish beneath the rising waters, as ocean shorelines almost everywhere recede. A world is in transformation, and with it a way of life.

The Paleolithic Age closed with the final melting of the great ice sheaths that had alternately advanced into and retreated from the world's temperate zones during periods of cooling and warming. As the ice departed, a new world came into view. The great herds of huge herbivores, thinning for millennia, finally disappeared, victims of climate change, overhunting, disease, or a combination of the three. The return of forests to long treeless reaches, the flowering of equatorial deserts, and the spread of plant and animal species opened a new age of opportunity for human observation and invention.

Two Bands

Four thousand years later, two slightly larger bands meet at a summer encampment, an expression of the slowly emerging tribal social order. The two bands gather for what is likely the last time. Though both descend from the group that made its cautious trek along the ice cliffs millennia before, their pathways have begun to diverge. One still lives by the older ways we know as Paleolithic, following the vanishing herds of large ice-age mammals—the mammoth they most prize. Their lifeways and technology are intimately bound up with the hunting of the great beasts. Skilled gatherers, they have developed a range of taxonomical skills that have served them well in this familiar landscape.

But the great herds are sighted less often now. As the ice melts, the mammoth, the steppe bison, the cave bear, the horse, and other big game animals first flee northward and then begin to disappear. Slowly, Paleolithic human culture fades as well. The climatic shift that steamed away the ice sheaths has also produced dramatic changes in the zones and seasons that govern plant life. But at the same time, the changing environment is combining with human innovation to set the stage for the most important single cultural stride in human history, the "Neolithic Revolution." A new horizon is opening: the shift from an economy based on hunting and gathering to one primarily concerned with the production of food. And a cultural explosion will follow: permanent settlements, storage and distribution of food, craft specialization, public works, and, in time, the rise of urban civilization.

As the change unfolds, members of the Paleolithic group continue to live their short lives in accord with a cultural pattern that has persisted for a million and a half years. They have largely resisted the pull of the new wave. The band collects seeds only for consumption, never for planting; its members domesticate no animals; and its flint knappers have scarcely enlarged their toolkit. Only a few have even begun to suspect that their customs are slowly becoming irrelevant.

The second band, still Paleolithic in most of its fundamental assumptions and values, is nevertheless beginning a new life, blessed by the vision of three remarkable individuals: a hunter who understands that the great herds of huge animals will one day be gone and that the group must now learn to hunt further down the food chain; a knapper who has begun to shape a rich new repertoire of tools of stone, bone, and wood; and a farsighted woman—a scientist we might call her—whose careful observation and experimentation now help to open the path from gathering to gardening and finally to agriculture.

Each of the visionaries has become aware of the changing environmental and economic realities—the anomalies—that demand a new way of living. And the long, slow transition begins, to the period that will be known as the Neolithic (the New Stone Age). To our two imagined bands, however, the transition seems astonishingly rapid, and it will make for a tension-filled summer gathering.

Settling Down

The domestication of plants and animals was off to a propitious early start by ten thousand years ago in the lands watered by the Tigris, Euphrates, and Nile rivers. The region that history knows as the Fertile Crescent was marginal by the standards of modern agriculture; nevertheless, in time it would host a rich variety of domesticable edible plants and an array of animals suitable for taming. In time, at least five independent centers of plant and animal domestication, gardening, and later agriculture would emerge from China to the Americas, but none would equal the abundance of the Mesopotamian garden. The collectors of wild plants who eventually turned to simple gardening could not have imagined the farmer's ultimate impact—the heart of the Neolithic Revolution. The first tamer of a large herbivore would never know how that simple act would transform the world that created the wheel.

The extraordinary shift to sedentary agriculture yielded population increase, food surpluses, craft specialization, technological development, writing, and more complex social organization. The common—and inaccurate—belief is that the adoption of the sedentary agrarian life came about because the farmer could make a living more easily than the hunter-gatherer. In fact, nomadic existence offered far more leisure time but became far less reliable as the herds declined and human populations began to expand. That expansion combined with the development of skillful food production in a positive feedback loop that enabled explosive human growth and ensured the spread of the agricultural lifestyle.

As Jared Diamond writes in *Guns, Germs and Steel,* "Plant and animal domestication meant much more food and hence much denser human populations. The resulting food surpluses and (in some areas) the animal-based means of transporting those surpluses, were a prerequisite for the development of settled, politically centralized, socially stratified, economically complex, technologically innovative societies."[1]

Population increase and the spread of many innovations we associate with civilization (writing, the wheel, etc.) helped the Neolithic paradigm prevail. Stonehenge and the Great Pyramid speak volumes about the earliest sea change, since these monuments of civilization could have been created only by a culture that had mastered centralized production and storage of food.

Change and Resistance: The Religious Crossing

Like all sea changes, the Neolithic wave almost certainly generated its mix of yeasayers and naysayers. In these rare periods of accelerated cultural change, advocates of new values clash with the adherents of older ways. Complex infrastructures of change and resistance come into play. In the arena of religion and spirituality, value networks associated with the old wave and newer wave are often more easily observable. Though we can only make an educated guess, we might reconstruct the religious dynamics of the Paleo-to-Neo crossing as follows.

Group identity was in transition. If, for example, a band's principal mode of subsistence was hunting mammoths, its shelters were constructed with the tusks, bones, hides, teeth, and sinews of the great pachyderms. The group's ritual life and its essential identity were shaped by the comings and goings of the herds. The shaman's spiritual communion with the grandfather or grandmother mammoth provided the tribe's most essential link to deep reality. Coming-of-age ceremonies certainly revolved around the hunt. Now, however, myths and rituals had to be reconceived. New religious actors took the stage.

Gender roles changed as knowledge of seeds and gardening came into its own. For some, the shift of focus to lesser game and to planting must have seemed an abandonment of the holy itself, a betrayal of life's central mystery: the delicate partnership between human and mammoth. How did members of other bands still faithful to the old ways regard the apostates?

That's just one of the unanswered questions that attend the earliest known sea change. Countless others exist: What moral and social eddies resisted the culture change? For how long? Did estrangements that attended the shift to new lifeways ever result in violence? Does the tale of Cain and Abel (which may have Sumerian roots) reflect the ancient tension between nomadic herdsmen (closer to their hunter-gather ancestors) and the settled farmers?

AT THE AXIS: THE SECOND SEA CHANGE

Our next setting is still an ancient time, some three thousand years ago. Another cultural upheaval is about to convulse the established order. What later scholars will term "civilizational religion" has dominated the known world for over two millennia, but a new religious and cultural wave is building. Wandering philosophers and religious thinkers are exploring fresh ideas, while experimental religious communities—cults at the fringes of the great empires—are testing the spiritual and ethical dimensions of human life. From these roots will grow the great classical religious edifices of India, China, the Middle East, and ultimately Europe. The upheaval is a cultural sea change, the second in the series of three on the way to our own. Theologian Ewert Cousins described its impact:

> Although the leaders who effected this change were philosophers and religious teachers, the change was so radical that it affected all aspects of culture, for it transformed consciousness itself. It was within the horizons of this form of consciousness that the great civilizations of the

Middle East, Asia, and Europe developed. Although within these horizons many developments occurred through the subsequent centuries, the horizons themselves did not change. It was this form of consciousness that spread to other regions through migrations and explorations, thus becoming the dominant, though not exclusive, form of consciousness in the world. To this day, whether we have been born and raised in the culture of China, India, Europe, or the Americas, we bear the structure of consciousness that was shaped in this Axial Period.[2]

Jaspers' Crossing

Imagine a little café somewhere in the Old World in the sixth century BCE. We sit and watch as some rather remarkable luminaries stroll in. Zoroaster, Jeremiah and Ezekiel, Thales and Anaximander, Mahavira, Uddalaka, Siddhartha the Buddha, Lao-tzu and Confucius all arrive and begin to converse. Impossible? Almost certainly. But the gathering is at least conceivable, for each of these architects of the modern religious edifice may have lived in the extraordinary sixth century BCE.

The great German philosopher Karl Jaspers, in *The Origin and Goal of History*, first called attention to what he termed an "Axial Period" in human culture and civilization, a turbulent time in China, India, and the West (the Middle East) that, he argued, "gave birth to everything which, since then, man has been able to be." Throughout the first millennium BCE, human societies from China to the Middle East began to take up their own versions of questions that would soon be universal: Who are we? Where do we come from? Why do we exist? How should we live? Jaspers offers a summary of the emerging process:

What is new about this age, in all three areas of the world, is that man becomes conscious of Being as a whole, of himself and his limitations. He experiences the terror of the world and his own powerlessness. He asks radical questions. Face to face with the void he strives for liberation and redemption. By consciously recognizing his limits he sets himself the highest goals. He experiences absoluteness in the depths of selfhood and in the lucidity of transcendence. . . .

In this age were born the fundamental categories within which we still think today, and the beginnings of the world religions, by which human beings still live, were created. The step into universality was taken in every sense.[3]

Civilizational Religion: The State and the Temple

In the last millennium BCE, the period of the great ancient empires was winding down and with it the age of civilizational religion, the religion of the state. Each of the great temples served a pantheon of gods and goddesses whose powers and whims were of direct consequence to the state and its ruler. Battle, planting and harvest, the weather, the river's flooding, and the well-being of the ruler—these were the critical religious themes of the civilizational religious order. Personal spirituality and the problems of human ethical behavior were not significant concerns.

The ruler was the chief religious actor, and it was *his* afterlife that was at issue, rather than that of the ordinary individual. The rich burials of pharaohs and the spectacular terracotta army that accompanied China's emperor Shin-shih Huang-ti into death testified to the divine existence that awaited the god-kings.

Significant also is that, while the rulers were imperial in their worldview, the consciousness of the ruled was still largely tribal. Their cultures were wedded to the mythic cosmos and depended on harmony with nature and the mythic songs and stories that described its cycles of fertility, creation, destruction, and renewal.

Existential concerns were, nevertheless, beginning to emerge in human culture. Anomalies multiplied: the failure of royal promises, ever-more-apparent human misery, the multiplication of contradictions linked to concerns for personal identity and deliverance. The most familiar anomaly took form in the questions, What's in it for me? How am *I* to live, to understand my place in a changing world order, to reconcile with death? Why am *I* here? What is the spiritual dimension of *my own* existence?

The decline of the imperial period in Sumer, Egypt, and China was accompanied by the rise of cultic centers on the peripheries. New ideas took root in the fecund decay of civilizations. The pattern was clear. Anomalies became undeniable and alternative models began to emerge. Everywhere, individual consciousness began to distinguish itself from the tribal mind-set.

> The Axial Period ushered in a radically new form of consciousness. Whereas primal consciousness was tribal, Axial consciousness was individual. "Know thyself" became the watchword of Greece; the Upanishads identified the *atman*, the transcendent center of the self. The Buddha charted the way of individual enlightenment; the Jewish prophets awakened individual moral responsibility. This sense of individual identity, as distinct from the tribe and from nature, is the most characteristic mark of Axial consciousness. From this flow other characteristics: consciousness that is self-reflective, analytic, and that can be applied to nature in the form of scientific theories, to society in the form of social critique, to knowledge in the form of philosophy, to religion in the form of mapping an individual spiritual journey. This self-reflective, analytic, critical consciousness stood in sharp contrast to primal mythic and ritualistic consciousness.[4]

The Amazing Sixth Century

In the sixth century BCE, an unprecedented convergence of visionaries emerged. In three regions of the Old World, new spiritual teachings came to light, each addressing the new concerns of individual seekers.

The ancient Chinese contributed the mythic vision of the tension between the masculine, ordering yang and the feminine, nurturing yin—the two great poles of Chinese religious thought, one inspired by the teachings of Master K'ung-Fu-tzu (Confucius) and the other by stanzas attributed to the mysterious Lao-tzu, founder of Chinese Taoism.

India added the literature of the Upanishads to the Axial ferment as Hinduism stepped forth from the background of Indian sacrificial religious ritual. These texts embraced the new guru-disciple paradigm that would shape Hindu and later Buddhist spirituality. Soon, Indian religion discovered the power of devotion to an incarnation of the transcendent divine as the figure of Krishna took the religious stage. In the same pivotal sixth century, Mahavira, the great teacher of Jainism, brought the teaching of *ahimsa*, "non-injury," to all living creatures. And Siddhartha Gautama, the Buddha, shaped the dharma, the Buddhist teachings of compassion and enlightenment.

In sixth-century Persia, the philosopher and religious reformer Zoroaster (Zarathushtra) championed a monotheism tempered by the powerful tension between good and evil in the universe.

The century also brought the high point of the great Jewish prophetic tradition in the persons of Jeremiah and Ezekiel. The prophetic demand for social justice that took shape during this period would help form the ethical character of Judaism, Christianity, and Islam.

Greek philosophy and science also arose in the sixth century, in the great movement known as the Ionian or Milesian school. Thales, Anaximander, and Anaximenes dedicated their considerable intellectual energies to discovering a single natural element (water, fire, earth, air) that underlay all of nature and existence. They were followed by the great natural philosophers Heraclitus and Pythagoras and the three most influential figures in Greek thought, Socrates, Plato, and Aristotle.

The Axial Legacy

Jaspers' model describes a monumental sea change in human culture—the crossing from mythical consciousness to rational, reflective consciousness. It also reveals the shift from temple-state religions to classical philosophical and religious systems. The ascending wave produced countless new cultic expressions, each reflecting on the individual's place in the cosmic scheme in terms of spirituality, ethics, and identity.

Reflect on the Axial turning and you can see the gradually emerging mindsets of the transition, including:

- awareness of the world, the cosmos, as a reality entire;

- attention to a unitary God or core principle of the cosmos;

- a new sense of the human individual as related to the overarching whole;

- exploration of the self and consciousness;

- the focus on human mortality and on salvation, liberation, or redemption;

- a new focus on ethics, individual responsibility for the other, justice;

- reflection on the transcendent and the nature of ultimate reality.

The Resistance?

How did the two cultural waves interact? There must have been eddies—organized patterns of resistance to the newer wave. And a conservative reaction did indeed emerge. By their nature, eddies challenge the rising newer wave by intensifying or narrowing older values. Skepticism, serious doubt, or confusion results.

Many stories survive that hint at cultural tensions marking the period when the two great culture waves crossed. Tales abound of dialogues and disputes between sages and emperors: Joseph or Moses and Pharaoh; parallel Indian and Chinese tales; or the classic Buddhist text, the *Milindapanha* (The Questions of King Milinda), about the encounter between a wise Buddhist master and a skeptical local ruler. Taoists tell how the initial failure of the legendary Lao-tzu to persuade others (and the emperor in particular) of his insights led to his departure from the realm, delayed by the warden of the gate long enough to allow him to set his thoughts down in a book of five thousand characters.

The trial of Socrates pitted the teacher of the new wisdom against the guardians of the received truths of the older order, with the inevitable result of a verdict of blasphemy and a sentence of death. The clashes between Egypt and later Rome and their fractious monotheists—Jews and Christians—also testify to the violence that attended the Axial culture break. Christian Gospel accounts of the last hours of Jesus portray him as a perceived threat to the established tribal order of the Hebrew temple cult (not yet overcome by the Axial transition represented by Jeremiah and Ezekiel) *and* to Roman imperial power. The second crossing was for many a religious trial.

Copernicus's Planetquake: The Third Sea Change

The three most familiar manifestations of the last sea change prior to our own were the Renaissance, the Protestant Reformation, and the Scientific Revolution. But we often associate the entire crossing with the vision of a single man.

In 1543 Nicolaus Copernicus published his masterwork, *De Revolutionibus Orbium Coelestium*, and the world was about to change. He knew his Sun-centered model of the cosmos was daring and even dangerous, but he had no idea of the changes his ideas would summon forth. The Polish mathematician and sky watcher had the audacity to proclaim that the Earth is not the unmoving center of the universe, although everyone *knew* it to be so. Instead, he declared, our world is a mere "planet" (from the Greek for "wanderer"), an insignificant denizen of the system of worlds moving in stately circular orbits around the Sun. Our universe is not *geocentric* but heliocentric.

From a cultural evolutionary perspective, the real significance of Copernicus is his work's challenge to Ptolemy's long-accepted doctrine of an Earth-centered universe and to Aristotle's notion of Earth's immovability. Since the high Middle Ages, the church had sanctioned both viewpoints. Now a mere natural philosopher had dared to insist that the great Aristotle and the authority of the church were in error.

"The Sun is Lost . . ."

In the fifty years following the astronomer's death, very few members of the educated classes in Europe placed much credence in his theories. His radical approach, however, embodied the spirit of the new science that would soon transform the Western intellectual establishment. Only by understanding how a fundamental flaw of such proportions weakened the prevailing worldview can one appreciate the enormity of the sixteenth century's eddies of reaction. Resistance to the Copernican theory was enormous, and this sixteenth-century eddy is worth dwelling on, revealing how segments of society cling to the old worldview.

The Aristotelian and Ptolemaic systems had insisted on the fixity of the Earth at the center of the universe, with the Sun, Moon, and planets in circular orbits around it. Copernicus offered instead the seemingly absurd proposal that the Sun was the fixed center of the planetary system and the Earth revolved around that center. Since physical experience seemed to contradict the notion of a moving Earth and since the older systems explained much that the Copernican model could not yet account for, the intellectual establishment refused to consider seriously the new Sun-centered theory.

Many ordinary believers were shocked that the Earth might not be the focal point of creation. To assert that the Earth wanders with the other planets in an incomprehensibly vast universe seemed to dethrone the Creator. Who could accept that the magnificent drama of Christ's Redemption of fallen humankind had been played out in an insignificant corner of the universe?

Although the new theory fit much more elegantly with observable data than the Ptolemaic and Aristotelian models, some churchmen, scholars, and even poets were aghast. How could something so contrary to tradition, observation, and intuition possibly be true? As John Donne put it, in his famous lament "An Anatomie of the World":

> *And new philosophy calls all in doubt,*
> *The element of fire is quite put out;*
> *The sun is lost, and th'earth, and no man's wit*
> *Can well direct him where to look for it.*
> *And freely men confess that this world's spent,*
> *When in the planets and the firmament*
> *They seek so many new; they see that this*
> *Is crumbled out again to his atomies.*
> *'Tis all in pieces, all coherence gone;*
> *All just supply, and all relation.*[5]

Donne, like so many other intellectuals, leaders, and ordinary people of the sixteenth and early seventeenth centuries, felt that the new science diminished not only the Earth but humanity, from "crown of creation" to meaningless speck on a wandering orb. Jean Bodin, one of the leading political thinkers of the sixteenth century, expressed the learned disdain of medieval culture for the upstart hypothesis:

No one in his senses, or imbued with the slightest knowledge of physics, will ever think that the earth, heavy and unwieldy from its own weight and mass, staggers up and down around its own center and that of the sun; for at the slightest jar of the earth, we would see cities and fortresses, towns and mountains thrown down. . . . For if the earth were to be moved, *neither* an arrow shot straight up, nor a stone dropped from the top of a tower would fall perpendicularly, but either ahead or behind. . . . Lastly, all things on finding places suitable to their natures, remain there, as Aristotle writes: Since therefore the earth has been allotted a place fitting its own nature, it cannot be whirled around by other motion than its own.[6]

Others, however, sensed that something profound and vital was stirring. Considering the demands the new planetary hypothesis placed upon sixteenth-century common sense, the establishment's intellectual hesitation is not surprising. Still, the elegance and mathematical precision of the new model captured the imagination of a perceptive minority. In time, interest in the thought of Copernicus developed until the great Italian scholar, astronomer, and mathematician Galileo Galilei emerged as the catalyst that would make the Copernican Revolution a reality.

The Crossing to Modernity

Long convinced of the validity of the Copernican model of the universe, Galileo Galilei (d. 1642) amassed a great deal of data that uniformly suggested the correctness of the new theory. Finally, in 1611, he visited Rome, where he demonstrated his remarkable new telescope and received an enthusiastic response at the papal court. Encouraged, he began to express his views more openly, citing especially the apparent movement of "sunspots" as evidence of the real movement of the Earth. For a time, it appeared as though the eloquent Galileo would carry the day. The universities of Europe witnessed tremendous growth of interest in the new ideas, and significant popular support began to build. However, the Aristotelians who dominated the intellectual climate of the early seventeenth century rightly viewed Galileo as a threat to the hegemony and, therefore, to the structure of the philosophical and theological establishment.

The opposition organized very quickly. Dominican preachers railed against the apparent clash of the Copernican-Galilean model with the tenets of scripture. Galileo was denounced to the Inquisition as a blasphemer. Although his critics cited the authority of scripture in their attacks on Galileo, the apparent conflict of his system with revelation was not their primary concern.

The real problem was that the older cosmology set the eternal celestial realm in opposition to the terrestrial scene of change and decay. The hierarchical "chain of being" approached perfection as it moved from the material toward the divine. The new cosmology obliterated this distinction between the corruptible and the incorruptible; it applied uniform natural categories to the whole universe. The great theological structure of significance was placed in jeopardy. In particular, the place of human beings was demoted from the center of the universe to a spinning, peripheral planet. Many Renaissance thinkers saw the new thinking as enhancing rather than diminishing the status of the human; many others, however, believed that the uniqueness of humankind and the idea of God's particular concern for Earth seemed in danger.

Finally, in 1616, the Copernican theory was condemned, and the authorities warned not to continue to expound the now-forbidden doctrine. Some seventeen years later, with church authorization, Galileo completed his *Dialogue Concerning the Two Chief World Systems*, a comparison of the Ptolemaic and Copernican views. While he had complied with the terms of the official permission, prefacing and concluding his work with statements to the effect that humans cannot know how God really created the world or what the world is really like, his demonstration of the superiority of the Copernican model proved so compelling that it excited a storm of renewed interest.

Galileo was once again summoned to Rome. On this occasion, he stood trial and was convicted. He was forced to recant the ideas whose correctness he had so convincingly demonstrated. Despite the tremendous bulwark of opposition Galileo faced, in his person the revolution became a reality, and the challenge raised so unsuccessfully by Copernicus became a serious affront to the powers-that-be.

To the Copernican model Galileo had added a functioning mechanical analysis that solved many of the critical problems of the earlier forms of the theory. This accomplishment, later completed by Kepler's revision of the planetary scheme in terms of the real elliptical orbits of the heavenly bodies, cleared the way for Isaac Newton's enunciation of the laws of motion and the theory of gravitation. The eventual acceptance of the Copernican system was a certainty, and the Scientific Revolution was underway.

In the years of his struggle, Galileo sharply defined the new scientific attitude, legitimizing the study of nature: "I think that in discussions of physical problems we ought to begin not from the authority of Scriptural passages but from sense-experience and necessary demonstrations, for the holy Bible and the phenomena of nature proceed alike from the divine Word."[7]

Galileo's most significant contribution, then, was this: mathematics holds the key to understanding. By demonstrating the power of mathematical inquiry and modeling, he raised mathematics from the status of an art to that of a true science, able to effect the transformation of the concrete into the abstract. A. R. Hall, the noted historian of science and technology, sums it up well: "Archimedes, Galileo's model, had submitted statics to geometry. But no one before had extended the mathematical model of reasoning to the motions of real bodies, nor been so bold as to declare that this method was valid through the whole range of physics: that indeed it was the only valid method. For to

Galileo, the mathematical method alone offered certainty of proof. . . . The architecture of the real world was no less geometrical that that of abstract Euclidean space. Nor was there any distinction between 'real truth' and mathematical truth."[8]

LOOKING BACK

Why is it so valuable to reflect on three preceding sea changes? The point of course is that their rhythms are so similar, despite the fact that their realities are so strikingly different. In each case an older set of values that once served society well has begun to lose influence. New life conditions have arisen, and basic understandings of the world and the human condition have changed. Anomalies appear, demonstrating the growing inadequacy of older assumptions; but soon, new insights— *ahas*—emerge, and a value shift is underway. It's particularly instructive to note that resistance to change always forms. Eddies inevitably arise. Their power, however, is easily overestimated. In the early stages of the Scientific Revolution, for example, the church seemed poised to crush any advance, but within three generations Europe's intellectual order had clearly accepted the new planetary system. The power of the onrushing wave makes its eventual ascent to dominance almost inevitable.

And now the modern adventure was underway. Every sea change advances humankind along the cultural evolutionary spiral. Each, of course, contains the seeds of its own decline and the rise of the next. In the next chapter, we'll touch on the best and worst of the modern value wave and, finally, ask what went wrong.

I am prisoner of a gaudy and unlivable present, where all forms of human society have reached an extreme of their cycle and there is no imagining what new forms they may assume.

—Italo Calvino, *Invisible Cities*

But with the rise of modernity, the spheres of art, science, and morals were clearly differentiated, and this marked the dignity of modernity because each sphere could now pursue its own truth without violence and domination from the others. . . . Modernity obviously has its own share of horrible problems. In fact, some of modernity's differentiations did go too far, into a specific set of dissociations—and those dissociations I refer to as the disaster of modernity. . . . This was indeed a disaster, a pathology, for it very soon allowed a powerful monological science to colonize and dominate the other spheres. . . . If differentiation was the dignity of modernity, dissociation was the disaster.

—Ken Wilber, *The Marriage of Sense and Soul*

5

Modernity: How Can a Sea Change Go Wrong?

Modernity's promise was fulfilled in countless ways, but the liberation of the personal and the objective from the tyranny of the collective was the great modern crossing. Individuality emerged, if not unfettered, at least with a relative degree of freedom. In its wake came the most celebrated advances of the modern era—in art, science, health, material prosperity, political democracy, human rights, global governance, and communication. But the modern age—like all sea changes—eventually went from good to bad. Actually, as we'll discover, things had to take the turn for the worse in order to move on to the next evolutionary stage.

For now, though, the question is, how could the ascendancy of the modern wave—the period of its triumph—give way to its decline? What were the critical stages of this process and how did it begin? Let's consider the essential stages of every sea change and then move on to the decline of the modern.

CHAPTER 5

PROGRESS AND PATHOS

Major evolutionary shifts arise when a culture's assumptions clash with people's life experiences. As the gap between expectation and reality widens, a critical cultural mass is reached. At the same time, new possible futures begin to appear. As anomalies and *ahas* surface, smaller paradigm shifts proliferate. Soon, an authentic sea change may be underway, and the two-wave process will commence. The discussion that follows applies to all sea changes but bears particularly on the rise and decline of the modern value system and the counter-rise of the twenty-first-century wave.

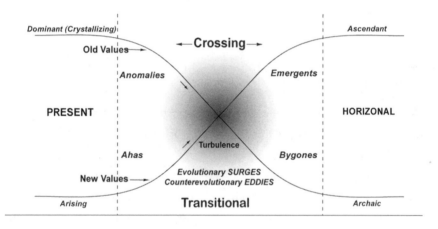

Figure 5.1. Sea Change: The Two Waves

Every sea change passes through several stages, from rise to decline. That doesn't mean the process is not evolutionary. Each completed value shift moves human culture further along the path toward greater complexity, interdependence, and integration of knowledge. The two-wave graphic suggests an up-and-down cycle, but it needs to be visualized on an ascending axis. In other words, it is a spiral.

Still, the wave movement has a sequence. Every period of major cultural advance must come to an end. The evolutionary spiral steadily ascends, but each major rising wave will eventually stabilize, coalesce, and then decline, engendering its own countervailing surge. The expanded two-wave graphic gives a more detailed view of the process by outlining the key periods of a sea change.

The figure centers on the most exciting moment of a sweeping cultural transformation: the imaginary instant at which the declining influence of the older culture and the rising momentum of the newer are equally matched. The animating question of this book remains, what might it mean to live at that moment of crossing?

The left dashed vertical line in the graphic represents the onset of cultural recognition that something significant is underway. The dawn of awareness at the beginning of the last sea change was certainly in the fifteenth-century Italian Renaissance, perhaps at the time of Pico della Mirandola's *Oration on the Dignity of Man*, the manifesto of the Renaissance. The second vertical of the last shift—marking the opening moment of modernity's ascendancy—lies somewhere in the late nineteenth-century embrace of the new science. My personal choice would be the 1875 address in which the president of the French Academy of Science intoned, "By 1925, we shall know everything."

The wave dynamic of our own sea change first began to come into focus in the tumultuous 1960s, when so much seemed suddenly in flux. Where the right vertical line lies—marking the beginning of the new wave's ascendancy—we just can't say.

Fall and Rise

The slowly accelerating decline of the present culture's dominant values makes way for a nearly simultaneous arising of a newer set of principles. The initial phase of the decline is rich with anomalies, unexpected contradictions of prevailing assumptions. While anomalies at first seem to be harbingers of chaos, they actually become centers of creative energy.

Think of anomalies as the ways in which the prevailing system begins to broadcast its essential flaws. Further, consider that these flaws catalyze a creative response: Where did we go wrong? How can our deepest core values make things better?

In the first of the two questions lies the key to cultural evolution. Anomalies give rise to *ahas*. We begin to question, and then we begin to wonder, to imagine, and to discover alternatives. When reality disappoints our expectations, we challenge predominant values. The dance of anomalies and *ahas* provides the essential energy of a sea change. The buildup of incongruities on one hand and new lucidities on the other means that the shift has commenced. But as we cross the first vertical line, the influence of the rising wave has not yet begun to rival the real power of the established older value wave.

Ascendancy

The more dramatic the decline in what we were sure was true, the greater the impact of disturbing new ideas. But why do the once-transformative new ideas of the last sea change seem to lose their magic? Why do the good ideas go wrong? Again, the question goes to the heart of cultural evolution.

As a culture shift progresses, a rising wave flattens into a comfortable *ascendancy*. Its preeminent new values become the accepted values of the culture. And this acceptance is, without question, the most directly evolutionary stage of the sea-change process.

As the medieval yielded to the modern, the latter came into its magnificent ascendancy. As greater numbers embraced the newer values, innovative initiatives were born and cultural creativity abounded. Comprehensive new understanding of natural philosophy gave rise to the sciences. Art and literature flourished. Feudalism failed. The Enlightenment seemed to promise a new intellectual order celebrating natural law, human rights, and the perfection of society. Many of the emerging principles hailed by the new moderns were authentic advances that survive today. Others would prove more troublesome.

Crystallization

Each new wave is dynamic initially, responding to subtle changes in human experience and understanding. But over time, a phase shift takes place. Just as water turns to ice, cultural motility diminishes. As *crystal-lizing* habit patterns and unexamined assumptions come to dominate cultural behavior, values give way to value judgments. Aspirations that were originally experimental become doctrinal standards and, finally, dogmatic certainties. The incoming wave slows, cools, and then freezes into ideological absolutes.

Penultimacy

The last stage of every sea change may be the most interesting. Each new wave, as it relaxes into dominance, births the next as a counterreaction. So it's worth inquiring into the penultimate—the next-to-last stage of each of our culture shifts.

Every major culture change culminates in the deterioration of once-revolutionary and flexible principles into established doctrines. In time, doctrines crystallize into authoritarian and ideological power structures. But the remedy incubates in the malady. Whatever the institution, the failure of a sufficient number of dogmatic canons energizes the next new wave.

The earliest of the great sea changes, the Paleolithic to Neolithic, produced centralization, specialization, and civilization. It culminated, however, and began its decline in the imperial era, whose anomalies brought forth the Axial Age, individual awareness, and the spiritual search. The crossing of fading Rome and rising Christianity is an instructive late exemplar of the Axial sea change.

The Axial Age itself came to rest in the late medieval period of religious triumphalism and ideological inflexibility. Art and natural philosophy were utterly subordinated to the religious establishment. And, of course, the multiplication of medieval anomalies and *ahas* birthed the resultant sea change.

The arrival of the modern age came with tremendous promise, but like the others, it carried the seeds of its own destruction.

Anomaly and Aha

Anomalies are the cultural outgrowth of—and the antidote to—values crystallization. Eventually, the crystallization of a culture's essential values prevents it from responding to new realities. Then, as time-honored assumptions begin to make less and less sense, strengthening anomalies reach a tipping point. A new wave begins to form. And new questions, born of anomalies, begin to generate culturally creative *ahas*.

Are women actually inferior? Is the Earth's resistance to human abuse truly inexhaustible? Can we actually ignore global human rights violations? Is war really built into the human condition? Well, perhaps not; let's think together.

The declining legitimacy of the assumptions of the older wave creates the space in which newer assumptions can emerge. For every premise that withers, an equivalent paradigm begins to emerge. The challenge phase, however, is the most contentious and, ultimately, the most dangerous. The period of crossing is attended by the rise of eddies of resistance as well as surges of change.

Evolutionary Surges

In our own time of transition, evidence that key modern certainties are invalid gives rise to a wide range of evolutionary surges—the seemingly sudden appearance of fertile new fields of inquiry and discovery. Among the most dramatic surges in the current values shift, for example, are human rights, ecological stewardship, empowerment of women, safety and education of children, global governance, integral knowledge, interreligious engagement, and spiritual growth. Each of these surges, however, gives rise to its own eddies of resentment and resistance.

Eddying

As the influence of the older wave declines and the rise of the next sea change becomes more evident, eddies form. Individuals and groups whose identities are thoroughly bound up with the older value complex intensify their investment in fading certainties. As older certainties face new evolutionary energies, eddies appear—vortices of resistance to change. Some of the most disturbing cultural patterns of our age belong neither to the older or the newer wave. Fundamentalism, fascism, greed, and hegemony, for example, are eddies—manifestations of the turbulent interaction of the two value waves.

Emergents

As the transitional stage—the crossing—draws to a close, the newer wave gives rise to often-surprising new forms. *Emergents* are the unlooked-for self-organizing patterns that shape much of cultural and biological evolution. In the context of a changing culture, they can bring new ways of thinking, new structures, and new modes of activism. A new wave is embodied in the emergent patterns it generates. From the networks of nongovernmental organizations to the surging popular support for human rights and environmental causes, emergence demonstrates the bottom-up power of cultural evolution.

CHAPTER 5

Bygones

What becomes of eroded certainties, when they have finally given up all real claims on redemption? They are the cultural evolutionary *bygones*. Some irretrievably erroneous notions are somehow never quite abandoned. They linger as pseudo-occult mysteries and hidden truths cherished somewhere: the cosmic spheres, the flat earth, the ether, the superior male, the pure race. And though still nursed along in cultic enclaves, they are bygone indeed, never really to return.

MODERNITY'S DIGNITY AND DISASTER

The philosopher Ken Wilber argues that the essential dignity of the modern age lay in its differentiation of the three estates of morals, art, and science. Prior to the extraordinary sixteenth-century confluence of the Renaissance, the Protestant Reformation, and the Scientific Revolution, the church dominated the other two spheres and limited their development. Differentiating the three modes of knowing brought the most celebrated advances of the modern era. But the modern age, like all sea changes, did not arrive unburdened.

As Wilber also notes, modernity tended to move from *differentiation* to *dissociation*. Once liberated from the hegemony of religion, the arts and sciences began to move further and further away from the moral sphere and from one another. Soon, science began to assume pride of place among the three disciplines. The overweening confidence of science rendered personal experience and cultural judgment largely irrelevant. If something could not be quantified, it wasn't worth exploring. Logic was not just a method, but the *only* one. In modernity's fealty to logic lay its undoing. Moderns saw the truth claims of the three estates as distinctly disparate. Soon, physical science would trump the other domains in all the most important questions.

You will recall the graphic from chapter 3 of Ken Wilber's Four Quadrant model of integral knowing (fig. 3.2, p. 70). Separating the hard from the social sciences, it represents the *three* estates as *four* distinct disciplines. All vital inquiries, Wilber argues, must be approached from all four vantage points. No single discipline exhausts what can be known.

Nevertheless, the intellectual hegemony of the upper right quadrant came to dominate the modern age. Still, that the postmodern denial of big narratives and absolute truths originated in architecture and art but eventually found secure bastions in literature and the social sciences is intriguing. Ironically, the struggle between absolute certainty and the suspicion of all certainties would emerge as modernity's philosophical endgame.

THE GOOD, THE BAD, THE UGLY . . . AND THE BEST

Ushered in by the sixteenth-century Copernican sea change, the era of modernity exemplified a passion for order, rationality, and assurance. Certainty and ambitious materialism provided modernity's cachet. Technological confidence powered it.

The complex modern wave lifted up ideals for the *good*. It shattered the constrictive hegemony of the church, freeing up science and the arts and making extraordinary advances possible in those domains. It engendered the inspiration of the Enlightenment and put an end to the tyranny of feudalism.

But modernity's gradual disconnect from reality began a slow descent from the good to the *bad* toward the *ugly*. The good values of a given evolutionary era are those embodying its essential promise. As the values that shape a culture become less flexible and less responsive to changing experience, they enter the bad stage. Finally, as authoritarianism replaces innovation and values become ideologically mired, we can identify the ugly marker of cultural stagnation. So it was with the modern era.

CHAPTER 5

By the mid-twentieth century, some of modernity's most established systemic assumptions (patriarchy, classism, racialism, and human dominance over nature) had become untenable. Deepening human understanding began to highlight the incongruous character of many common beliefs and behaviors and to call attention to the era's bad or even ugly side. Like all dominant value systems, modernity responded to the outcry over anomalies with an exercise of power. Contrarian voices were silenced or simply ignored.

The devolution from the good to the bad was straightforward. Kinship and religious belief easily yielded to nationalism and exclusivism. The right gave way to the expedient. The heroic became the self-righteous; the nurturing fatherhood, patriarchy; the patriotic, the chauvinistic; and the advocacy of law, corruption. In every case, the passage from the good to the bad meant an increase in inflexibility. The struggle for survival gave rise to a swaggering contempt for the natural order, and the benevolent community became obsessed with the enemy at the gate. What was once a broad range of inquiries slowly declined into a narrow system of certainties.

But the next devolutionary downspin was what turned things ugly. Certainties abide until a challenge arises. Under assault, they become socially unchallengeable. Bitter and sometimes violent patterns of resistance arose. In every category, the descent into the ugly meant the embrace of ideological absolutism: "Don't bother me with facts."

It would be a mistake, however, to conclude that a sea change abandons all the values and thought patterns that had shaped its once-rising wave. As we'll see, many of the deepest core values of modernity (for example, kinship, faith, individualism, patriotism, and the rule of law) continue to energize the new wave, though now transformed and differently expressed. Core values that survive the forces of crystallization and the lure of authoritarianism evolve and become the legacy of a sea change—the *best*. And that legacy shapes the core values of the next new wave.

Assault on the *Oikos*

The crystallization of the ethical and moral standards of the late modern period represents a collapse of the relationship to the human family and the Earth household. *Oikos*—Greek for "home," "household," or "family"—is the root of several key terms including ecology, economy, ecumene (the occupied world), and ecumenical (interreligious). As we all know, our modern world struggles with issues involving peace, social and economic justice, ecological sustainability, and harmony among the religions.

Consider, for example, modernity's relationship to nature: how we learned to use it for shelter, energy sources, health, and economy. With the passage of time, however, we began to take nature for granted. Worse, we failed to pay heed to the fragile balance between our needs and nature, resulting in negative consequences/anomalies: air and ocean poisoning, species extinction, and climate change. Only then did we start to understand and respect nature.

How did we moderns get into our predicament? Why haven't the promises of the modern world—a harmonious relationship with nature, for example—been fulfilled? It all began with the last sea change. The eighteenth-century Enlightenment—inspired by the Renaissance, the Reformation, and the Scientific Revolution—let art and science off the leash, freeing them from control by religion. (This was good.) In time, however, the sciences became dominant and dismissed the other ways of knowing as irrelevant. (This was bad.) The result was the dissociation of all the great disciplines—art, philosophy, religion, morality, culture, science, and technology. (When their exchanges ceased, things got ugly.) The cracks that began to appear in the modern façade—anomalies—resulted in significant measure from that imbalance.

As moderns learned that more and more accepted truths just didn't make sense, the modern tapestry began to fray. Imagine a series of headlines in a satiric publication like *The Onion*: Extra!!—Women Not Stupid;

Historians Discover that War Does Not Lead to Peace; Smoking No Longer Kool; Humans Declared Bad for Planet; Americans Astonished to Learn of World Hunger; or Scientists Say Can't Fix Global Problems. When anomaly yields to satire, a culture is well into its anomalous period.

Over the past half century, America witnessed the mutation of some of modernity's core values. Under pressure, good values had too often devolved into bad or ugly variants. While we slumbered, patriarchy had at times become angry sexism, individual freedom had yielded violence against groups, and humanity's triumph over nature had unleashed ecocide.

Let's look at various areas in which modernity has gone astray. As we'll see, anomalies gave rise to *ahas* in each. It seems we had to go from good to bad to ugly in order to bring out the best.

Religion and the Dark Side

Religion, as a source of inspiration and a repository of guiding principles, was a foundation stone of modernity. It was a good. At the turn into the twentieth century, however, fundamentalism took the stage. Its insistence on the literal and historical perfection of scripture set a collision course with science as the major competing repository of truth. By the early 1920s, the anti-evolutionist argument was taking shape. It burst forth in the 1925 Scopes trial. Humiliated by the machinations of H. L. Mencken and Clarence Darrow, fundamentalists retreated into the back-country of the young United States. When they reemerged, in the 1970s, the bad (literalist narrowing of the richness of the scriptural message) had turned ugly. Now fundamentalism was a worldwide phenomenon, employing the most modern methods to attack essential modern values. But the real target of religion's ugliest face, dominionism (manifest as Christianism, Islamism, Hindutva, etc.), was *not* modernity, but the rising evolutionary wave. Now small but powerful religious enclaves around the world set forth on missions of world domination.

Still, the most authentic critique of devolved religion came not from the atheist front but from the best and brightest within the religions themselves. Despite the pitfalls of exclusivism and fundamentalism, interreligious respect and interspiritual sharing emerged as the finest distillations of real religious inquiry.

Science's Problem: Scientism, Pseudoscience, Antiscience

Science is the blessing and the presenting problem of the modern sea change. Wilber's elaborate four-quadrant model shows the value of allowing each area to pursue its unique form of inquiry without interference. Science unchained was a very good thing, as Galileo clearly believed: "I do not feel obligated to believe that the same God who has endowed us with sense, reason, and intellect has intended us to forgo their use."[1]

The developing ability of science to identify areas of inquiry and then to frame and test hypotheses gave it a power no other discipline could rival. The individual artist or spiritual seeker could inspire but could not demonstrate the truth of a claim. Nor could the cultural disciplines of theology or philosophy prove the superiority of scripture or abstract reasoning over the scientific method. By the latter half of the nineteenth century, science had eclipsed philosophy, theology, spirituality, and the arts and seemed to most educated people the only true path to knowledge.

Scientific language, though, created barriers to understanding. Einstein's relativity theories and the later development of quantum mechanics took science forever beyond the reach of ordinary language and ability to visualize. Now only a very few could grasp the great truths and then only mathematically. The tendency was inevitable: scientific triumphalism—*scientism*—had arrived.

If liberated science was among modernity's founding goods, then scientism was an early and enduring bad. When science becomes ideological—as materialist fundamentalism—we've reached the ugly stage. Wilber noted: "Full of itself and flush with stunning victories, empirical science became scientism, the belief that there is no reality save that revealed by science, and no truth save that which science delivers."[2]

The nineteenth century spawned a plethora of pseudoscientific researches and claims, including phrenology, animal magnetism, spurious health treatments, and even antigravity machines. In the twentieth century, given its warrant by the anti-evolution movement (fundamentalism's pseudoscientific front line), the callow acceptance of unsupported scientific-sounding arguments took on a life of its own in the form of conspiracy theories, unhealthy health fads, bogus investigations into historical and scientific "mysteries," and the World Wide Web became a powerful legitimizer of unscientific nonsense.

Polls throughout the first decade of the twenty-first century have shocked many supporters of the scientific view of life and the universe. Twenty-five percent of Americans in one survey believed that the Sun makes a regular circuit of the Earth. Fifty-two percent think that the earliest humans lived alongside dinosaurs. Thirty-five percent think drinking radioactive milk is quite safe as long as it's been boiled. That's pseudoscience.

Even more alarming are the low numbers of respondents who support well-established scientific arguments for long-term biological evolution (about thirty percent) or anthropogenic climate change (about forty-five) percent. Intriguingly, the anti-evolutionary campaign in the United States and Europe employs pseudoscientific language to advance a distinctly antiscience agenda. The proliferation of new creationist museums attests to the power of science fakery in service to a radically antiscience agenda.

This ugly phase began as certain sectors of society moved beyond suspicion to organized denial. Demagogic manipulation, usually motivated by political rather than religious or philosophical concerns, has intruded into countless areas of the modern conversation about science.

The movement finds its most organized and insidious expressions in stem-cell "defense," the intelligent-design assault on biological science, and the carefully orchestrated mockery of a whole range of ecological issues ranging from biodiversity loss, to pollution of land, air, and water, to the most critical: climate change.

But in science, as in the other sectors, one of modernity's seminal goods developed into one of its best manifestations. The transitional phase of the twenty-first-century sea change has witnessed the late modern refinement of integral knowing—the reunification of the four quadrants—as a founding good of the new-wave revolution.

Pomos in the Academy

The American higher-education establishment has played contrasting roles with respect to modernity. While academics often embrace modern assumptions, they also challenge them. Politically left, philosophically relativist, and often deliberately obscurantist, the postmodernist revolution nevertheless brought a breath of fresh air to universities in Europe and the United States. It challenged the canons of literature and social science, calling into question the white male perspective. Scholars began to listen to the voices of women and people of color and to ask why they had been dispossessed. At times, the Pomo counterculture even dared to suggest that science itself had no real claim on absolute truth. The new openness, grounded in quintessentially modern multicultural awareness, was very good indeed. And, of course, it deteriorated.

In the last several decades of the twentieth century, universities turned from refreshing engagement with myriad voices to dialogue-stilling political correctness (bad). The ugliest manifestation was the denial of all absolutes. This position proceeds from the notion that no point of view has any inherent advantage over any other, that no intellectual position is "privileged." Consequently, we slide easily into relativism: no statement is absolutely true. Ironically, that statement is itself quite absolute.

Once again, however, the best of the modern age emerged from this ugly phase in the form of multicultural awareness. The old Hindu passage says it best: "Truth is one, but the sages know it by many names."[3]

Politics and Sound Bites

Originally, the term *sound bite* once meant the few words that best captured the sense of a longer statement. Mark Twain called it "a minimum of sound to a maximum of sense."[4] In an age in which critical discourse is too often dominated by negative political propaganda with little or no substance, *sound bite* has come to mean a minimum of substance with maximum volume.

The modern era was above all a celebration of political freedom. One of its essential goods found expression in greater human liberties and democratic experiments. The surely impossible American republic flourished and in the process witnessed several defining modern political struggles. In America, the four great struggles—for the rights of women, blacks, workers, and the poor—began a global contest for social and economic justice and human rights.

The bad came in the worldwide explosion of demagoguery. In America, the division of the new nation into states' rights and unionist parties gave way to identity resentment and populist political rage. Animosities generated in the American Civil War fueled conservative-liberal disputes throughout the Western world. And the ugly lifts its voice of fear and loathing from radio land to cyberspace, empowering populist distortions of the real problems facing America and the world.

To find the best in modern political reality, we turn to one of modernity's great accomplishments, the evolution of the idea of human rights through three generations. The first generation—individual civil rights—was foundational to American and European democratic experiments. The second—social-entitlement rights—was more controversial. Eventually the contest between first- and second-generation rights would define the right and left in the democratic political debate. Then came third-generation holistic or solidarity rights. If a rich northern country possessed technologies, health-care facilities, or energy resources that could benefit the poorer world, it was obligated to share. The call for the United States and other nations to make HIV-AIDS treatments available in Africa and elsewhere has been loud and sustained.

Social Transformation

Social transformation reveals more about sea change than any other sector. Is the basic community's evolutionary movement enclaving or all-embracing, elitist or communitarian? Is the community of the future homophobic, science-suspicious, mean-spirited, and dumbed down? Or is it world-centric, science-minded, openhearted, and inquiring? Society's bad turns have always been frightened and narrowing. Its ugliest have always gone the populist road of blaming others for its discomforts. Again, however, the best of modernity comes through. We stand on the threshold of becoming a world-embracing community, challenged by a new science and eager to embrace a new *horizontal* world.

And the Best

In parsing the good, bad, and ugly qualities of modernity's defining themes, we need to be aware of the fourth, the best. A culture's best values are the evolved forms of the good ones that churned up its sea change. The distilled best values of a culture call attention to the devolution of the good. They name the bad and the ugly. And—here's the real magic of cultural evolution—the best of the old wave emerges in the good values of the new. The continual reemerging of the best at the end of a cycle keeps cultural evolution churning. Figure 5.2 shows a few markers of the erosion and reemergence of some of modernity's core values.

Good	Bad	Ugly	Best
Kinship	Nationalism/ Racism	Ethnic Extremism	*World Centrism*
Religious Belief	Exclusivism	Fundamentalism	*Interspirituality*
Heroism	Self-Righteous Violence	Terrorism	*Nonviolent Conflict Resolution*
Individualism	Selfishness	Identity Politics	*Service*
Role of Father	Patriarchy/ Sexism	Intimate Violence	*Gender Equity*
Promoting Progeny	Homophobia	Gay Bashing	*Sexual-Orientation Equity*
Patriotism	Chauvinism	Neoimperialism	*Global Citizenship*
Surviving in Nature	Disregard of Nature	Ecocide	*Ecological Stewardship*
Evolving Human Rights	Socioeconomic Injustice	Systemic Abuse of Human Rights	*Civil Society and the Third Generation of Rights*
Community	Nation-States	Unipolarity	*Global Commons*
Law	Manipulation	Death of Civil Liberties	*Global Governance*
Laissez-faire Economics	Value-free Economics	Globalizing Greed	*The Virtuous Economy*
Multicultural Awareness	Postmodern Relativism	Death of Truth	*Pluralistic Truth*
Liberation of Art	What's Beauty?	No Beauty	*Beauty is Back*
Three Estates: Differentiation	Pseudoscience	Antiscience	*Rediscovery*
Liberation of Science	Scientism	Materialist Fundamentalism	*Integral Knowing*

Figure 5.2. The Good, the Bad, the Ugly, and the Best

MODERNITY: HOW CAN A SEA CHANGE GO WRONG?

We now turn our attention to our own sea change, its goods and their roots in the best of the modern age. Worth noting is how many of the characteristic tendencies associated with today's rising wave are strongly rooted in the resilience of modernity's best values.

The good news is the long-term trend of the past several centuries has been toward economic development, a process that has accelerated and spread around the world during the past few decades. Economic development seems conducive to the social and cultural conditions under which democracy is most likely to emerge and survive. . . . As we have seen, economic development is conducive to the spread of postmaterialist values, which give increasingly high priority to freedom of speech and political participation, and is linked with the emergence of relatively high levels of subjective well-being. In the long run, economic development tends to bring cultural changes that are conducive to democracy. These changes are part of a broader process linked with the emergence of post-modern values.

   —Ron Inglehart, "Globalization and Postmodern Values"

What is going to change? The prevailing societal trends of unlimited economic growth and material consumption will not continue, as they are not sustainable. On a global level, humanity will outgrow its adolescence, learning to become better stewards of Earth and its resources. Nations and cultures will increasingly come to honor each other as part of a global family, regardless of differences in race, religion, or nationality. Cooperation among nations will, out of necessity, begin to supersede conflict.

   —Edmund J. Bourne, *Global Shift*

6

Who Says It's
Getting Better?

My friend Wayne Teasdale was one of the major inspirations for this book. Though he knew about the project and loved it, he never fully understood his formative role. I regret that. Wayne, who died in 2004, was the most visionary spiritual thinker I have been privileged to know. He would have relished contributing his ideas to this book, especially this chapter. What *is* the new wave? He had a clear idea about that, and he was convinced that the new wave was advancing.

So I begin here with an insight offered by this extraordinary man (author of *The Mystic Heart*, *A Monk in the World*, and so many other books). "So many of the wars in history, thousands and thousands of them for the past five thousand years, have been related to differences in Truth claims. If we can evolve beyond that problem, then I think there's some chance that we could retire the whole institution of war and begin to focus on the peaceful evolution of humanity."[1]

Wayne's optimistic perspective sets the tone for this chapter, which examines our current sea change. We begin with a brief assessment of the period and place that marked the first real awareness of a cultural shift underway: the 1960s in America. What were the anomalies and *ahas* that heralded the horizonal sea change? And when did they first intrude upon our collective awareness? Unlike other sea changes, this was one I was in on from the start, so let me share my personal perspective.

THE AQUARIANS

Even today, people argue about the "good sixties" versus the "bad sixties." It was the time of my own coming of age, but only now do I understand why my inner debate about the period was so long unresolved.

The sixties were not the period of the ascendancy of a new wave, as we then fervently believed. They were instead the period in which the crystallization of the older wave became increasingly apparent. Since anomaly always slightly precedes *aha*, emergent new wave values take longer to manifest. Ours was a decade of problems recognized and solutions vaguely glimpsed, all set against turbulent events.

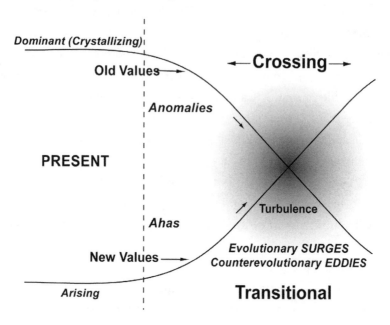

Figure 6.1. Crystallization of the Old and Ascent of the New

I spent a significant portion of 1968 as a foreign exchange student at the University of Leningrad. (Today Leningrad is once again St. Petersburg.) My Russian sojourn gave me a new appreciation of "the year that changed everything." (1968 brought devastating assassinations, the effective loss in Vietnam, the end of the LBJ years, and the beginning of a conservative political renaissance that would carry America through the Reagan presidency and beyond.)

I remember with particular clarity an evening spent with Russian friends discussing the war in Vietnam. Their opposition to the war was as sharp as my own, although their positions seemed based more on propaganda than reliable information. I was stunned by their reaction, however, when I mentioned that I was a conscientious objector. They were simply furious, demanding to know how one could "refuse to comply with what your country asks of you"? I later realized their reaction precisely mirrored the counterdemonstration taunts we endured at antiwar rallies. (My Russian friends were, however, considerably more polite.)

Today, the sixties controversy pits conservative veterans of the culture wars, like Harvey Mansfield and Pat Buchanan, against progressive veterans of the actual struggles that defined the decade. Tom Hayden recalls: "If anything, the '60s were a triumph for the notions of decentralized democratic movements championed in the Port Huron Statement [the defining declaration of the Students for a Democratic Society (SDS)]. Slogans like 'Let the people decide' were heartfelt. The powerful dynamics of the '60s could not have been 'harnessed' by any single structure; instead the heartbeat was expressed through countless innovative grass-roots networks that rose or fell based on voluntary initiative. The result was a vast change in public attitudes as the '60s became mainstreamed."[2]

This mythologized chapter in American life is significant to our inquiry in at least three ways:

- *The Incongruity*: The progressive members of the "Movement" clashed with the "Establishment" over the most destructive anomalies of the modern project: war; social, racial, and sexual inequality; ecological madness; and religious hypocrisy.

- *The Shape of Things to Come*: By the end of the decade, the seminal elements of the new wave could be clearly discerned. A flood of new ideas, new models, and new paradigms was unleashed. The *ahas* were much more influential than the all-too-obvious anomalies, though the negatives received most of the publicity.

- *Whirlpools*: Several of the most daunting eddies of resistance to cultural change in the early twenty-first century have a strong link to the sixties. Some began or enjoyed a significant development during that period (e.g., religious fundamentalism). Others would later define themselves in opposition to what they saw as an indulgent and destructive idyll (e.g., neoconservatism).

Not surprisingly, many yeasayers see the sixties as the source of the current value shift (the dawning of the Age of Aquarius), while naysayers often identify the decade with the beginning of a traumatic societal breakdown. While neither view is correct, the pro-sixties argument is closer to the mark; the period helped accelerate cultural-evolutionary sea change. And while the movement's promise exceeded its reach, it gave form to the young wave in words, images, and actions.

The 1960s witnessed the early signs of the oncoming sea change in music, the antiwar movement, and meditation. It was a time of international war and domestic violence, but also of scientific breakthrough and the exploration of outer space. The best-remembered and most controversial aspects of the sixties—civil rights, political, social, and ecological activism, communitarianism, the sexual revolution, and the spiritual quest—are now much easier to understand as harbingers of the more-developed evolutionary patterns that were to come.

New Age Coda

The New Age movement that began in the 1970s is different in many respects from its sixties' precursor. It was in many ways less a movement than a cult. Above all, the New Age movement needs to be understood in terms of approaches to power. In its earlier stages, it sought to find the sources of spiritual power. Later, it became fascinated with their exploitation.

One of the first thinkers to declare that a "new age" of spiritual and philosophical insight was approaching was Teilhard de Chardin. But how does one trace the passage from Teilhard to Shirley MacLaine and Oprah Winfrey? The answer lies in a series of juxtapositions that shaped the New Age movement as one of the most visible early forms emerging from the ferment of the sixties. Early on, the movement did not proclaim to know "the truth" but, rather, to know where to seek it—by bringing together what appeared to be pairs of opposites:

- ancient and modern

- East and West

- religion and philosophy

- spirituality and science

We'll return to the promise and paradox of the New Age movement later. It remains, however, one of the most enduring legacies of the first cultural stirring of the twenty-first-century sea change.

THE WAVELENGTH?

Discerning the wavelengths, the characteristic resonances of the earlier transitions, is easy enough. The rise to the Neolithic demanded a shift away from patterns of kinship to structures of active cooperation.

CHAPTER 6

The Axial was animated by the question of the meaning of life for the individual. The modern resonated with the power of intellectual analysis to generate truth, order, science, power, and wealth.

But what is the wavelength of our own sea change? Consider these critical shifts:

- from the personal to the communal

- from the communal to the global

- from the mechanical to the ecological

- from the intercultural to the planetary

Each is an indicator of a massive tectonic change. How much has the ground moved beneath our feet? In other words, how much has our understanding of reality altered over the four hundred years since the last sea change began? What value shifts are in the works, and how can we sort the progressive movements from the reactionary?

We need to explore two categories of cultural growth: what we see (our changing encounter with reality) and what we cherish (our evolving values). Let's begin with the evidence that our world is changing; then we'll move on to the new values that are taking shape.

What We See

In innumerable ways, modernity's accomplishments set the stage for the rise of the current sea change. As we've noted, though the good features of a rising wave may eventually crystallize and become distorted into bad or even ugly remnants, the best of any sea change survives into the next. The good ideas, insights, values, and behaviors of the rising wave are distillations of the best elements of the now-passing wave.

Know Thyself

Over the course of the modern period, our concept of the interior life of the self has changed radically. Our conception of the beautiful has broadened dramatically, making room for a multicultural aesthetic appreciation unimaginable even a century ago. The globalization of aesthetics has naturally produced a certain degree of mediocrity, but it has also brought the beauty of countless cultures within the reach of billions of people.

Something similar has happened in the domain of human spirituality. The opening up of long-isolated cultural approaches to spiritual growth has, as we'll see, deepened an important dimension of the planetary conversation. New approaches to inner experience have also emerged from psychology and the more authentic of the self-help movements. In many cases, the gulf that once separated psychology and spirituality has narrowed dramatically. In short, the early twenty-first century— particularly in the economically advantaged nations of the North— demonstrates a much greater degree of insight into the inner life than was true, say, a century ago.

Globalizing Culture

The modern period, arguably the bloodiest in human history, gave rise to genocidal totalitarianism and violent fundamentalism, yet it had another, far-better side. The rise of democracies around the world (although some were, to be sure, virtual shams) will long be regarded as one of modernity's most important contributions. At the same time, all over the world, even marginally educated people know far more today about the great challenges faced by the human community as a whole. We have, as a consequence of globalization, arrived at a point where more people on the planet know more about other peoples and cultures than ever before. To think of oneself as a "citizen of the world" has certainly become easier.

The Internet, too, has contributed to this global culture. Web 2.0, the next generation of Web design and development, has already opened up new pathways to creativity, interactivity, user-generated design, and the creation of virtual communities.

The Gift of Science

Modernity is most often assessed in terms of its signature scientific advances. Physics, chemistry, biology, geology, and the other major inquiries into "things" have brought about tremendous changes in our collective insight into the physical universe, the Earth, and the human condition.

Many of the activists who struggle daily to build a better world would argue, however, that modernity's scientific legacy has been more of a Pandora's box than a treasure chest. Their lament contains a good deal of truth. Self-proclaimed "value-free" science often wrought significant harm in the name of the untrammeled advance of knowledge. But at its best, today's science (the upper right quadrant in Wilber's chart) is indeed impartial, objective, and autonomous but no longer really value free. Most scientists would insist that a deep concern with key global challenges is clearly reflected in the selection of areas of research and the protocols of investigation. As Ed Rykiel, Environmental Science and Science Coordinator at Washington State University, puts it, "My viewpoint as a scientist is based on the question, What is the science? . . . My viewpoint as a citizen is based on the question, What are my values?"[3]

The World's Systems

We have witnessed an enrichment of the world's cultures, social and political systems, economies, religious teachings, and knowledge of its archaeological and anthropological roots, and geographical variety. The modern era transformed the movement of goods, services, money, cultural patterns, and information around the world. At the same time, it deepened and systematized our understanding of those processes through the social sciences.

The sea-change hypothesis itself depends in significant degree on evidence garnered in at least two centuries of broadening investigation of the world's cultures, social systems, and ecologies. Most valuable to the student of cultural evolution, however, is the rich variety of approaches to the question of the stages of human cultural evolution.

What We Cherish

What are the evolving values of the sea change we're living through today? At first, you may draw a blank, since we're often unaware of the changes taking place around us—people during the Renaissance remained unaware of its transformational role until it was quite advanced. Our own crossing, however, remains surprisingly unappreciated. What makes this a transformative time? Here are several defining markers:

- The movement from egocentrism through ethnocentrism to world centrism toward an emerging planet-centric identity: we have shifted over the course of several sea changes from caring about ourselves, to caring about our group, to caring about all humankind. The newest transition—to caring about all life—is a radical step. It's accompanied by a dramatic shift in our awareness of the larger world. My decisions affect and are affected by yours. I need to make my choices in the expansive context of a universe of countless interdependent life forms. We are not alone.

- The movement from the systematic models that characterized the modern age to the systemic approach that distinguishes our own: here's the difference. A systematic approach is organized, methodical, and often reductionist; it tends to stress the parts and to ignore the whole. A systemic model is holistic, concerned more with the functioning of the whole than with the identification and manipulation of the parts. Make no mistake, the systematic approach is often useful and even essential; but the systemic strategy can integrate any number of systematic models.

- The increased emphasis on spiritual growth: in our age, progressives drawn from a dozen different religious traditions or denominations have far more in common with one another than with fundamentalists within their own communities. The cross-cultural meeting point for progressives and pluralists is in shared spiritual insights. They may well continue to cherish their own doctrinal uniqueness, but a new respect for the spiritual paths of different cultures is a hallmark of the crossing.

- The three benchmarks themselves: the benchmark qualities—creative complexity, awareness of interdependence, and integral knowing—have clearly intensified in each of the three previous sea changes. In the twenty-first-century crossing, however, awareness of and conscious commitment to the benchmarks are far more pronounced than ever before.

THE GOOD, THE BEST, AND THE NEW

As a long-dominant values hierarchy begins to yield to a newer set, the rising value wave is an emergent phenomenon. The offspring of the older wave, it embodies many of its most fundamental principles. Advocates of the twenty-first-century new wave, for example, were weaned on the principles of peace, fairness, beauty, truth, and integrity. Those very modern ideals find their maturation in the new wave.

The new wave of a true sea change comprises a significant number of interdependent, mutually reinforcing themes. The growing disconnect between fading older values and the culture's newer spiritual, cultural, and scientific awareness creates value gaps. The themes that we will now explore are the goods that seem to be emerging to fill those gaps.

The power of cultural evolution, over millennia, lies in its uncanny ability to preserve the best of every cultural age, despite the turbulence of its passage from the scene. The rising goods of every new age are maturing forms of the best themes of the last. Remarkably, certain of the most important themes—egalitarianism, the feminine principle, the sacred Earth, the universal spiritual—can lose their luster for eons, only to reemerge evolved and reempowered.

All this begins to make sense when we recall the four dynamic processes that characterize all cultural evolution:

- complexity: the evolution of consciousness;
- chaos to order: how "open systems" advance;
- creativity: bottom-up, self-organizing, emergent forms; and
- cooperation: interdependence as evolutionary touchstone.

Properly understood, they offer a persuasive model of the process of cultural growth. We return to them now in the context of the twenty-first-century sea change.

THE HORIZONAL SHIFT

In the early twenty-first century, cultural evolution advances from the modern toward what we might call "the horizonal"—the values panorama just coming into view. From our vantage point near the epicenter of the event, we can provide a more detailed account of the sea change process.

In every sea change, the four dynamics intertwine in a perfect storm that reshapes every dimension of a cultural system. Cultures usually evolve steadily but slowly. Sea changes, though, are periods of "punctuated equilibrium" (to borrow a term from evolutionary biologists Stephen J. Gould and Niles Eldredge), dramatic forward leaps toward a closer fit between shared values and experienced reality.

As a consequence, sea changes are rare events. Printing presses, industrial revolutions, world wars, the invention of the computer, and the dawn of the Internet are not sea changes, but important paradigm shifts. Often, such significant developments play essential roles in a genuine sea change, but the latter is an all-encompassing transformation of all the dominant values of a culture, not just certain of its sectors or structures.

Steven Johnson is a pioneering explorer of self-organizing systems. His *The Invention of Air* muses about the link between important advances in understanding, on the one hand, and thoroughgoing cultural transformations, on the other. He writes about the phenomenon of the European Enlightenment, the culmination of the last sea change (the modern):

> There were literally dozens of paradigm shifts in distinct fields during [the period], watershed moments of sudden progress where new rules and frameworks of understanding emerged. . . .
>
> But what we don't have is a convincing theory about the system that connects all these local innovations, that causes them to self-organize into something so momentous that we have to dream up a name like the "Age of Enlightenment" to describe it. Beneath those local innovations some deeper force seems to be operating, a kind of intellectual plate tectonics driving a thousand tremors on the surface.[4]

We do, actually, have just such a theory. In a genuine sea change, countless independent variations in thought and action begin to converge and cross-pollinate. More complex patterns become more self-aware, more deliberate, and thus more likely to give rise to coherent emergent patterns. Value shifts are likely to be influenced by related *aha* experiences and thus to reinforce one another. As activists around the world have learned, the paths that lead to peace, justice, and ecological sustainability, for example, are intimately intertwined.

Every major component of a sea change is an expression of increased complexity, heightened conscious interdependence, and a change in what can be seen and acted upon in each of the four quadrants of integral knowing. The current sea change can be described in terms of several value shifts that have already arrived and a number of value complexes "whose time has come." Let's explore that distinction.

The *already emergents* are those value and behavior shifts that now exist and that make a strong argument for cultural evolution. Examples of already emergents include the decline of patriarchy, ecological awakening, and the rising awareness of human rights.

The *time-has-come* patterns are those just on the horizon, clearly apparent to yeasayers, largely imperceptible to the naysayers. The rhythm of their appearance charts the course of a period of heightened cultural evolution.

THE ALREADY EMERGENTS

One of the most persuasive arguments for cultural evolution in general and for our current acceleration resides in the emergents, manifestations of the new wave that are even now clearly observable. Testing shows each of the following emergents based on the three benchmarks to be authentic components of our current sea change:

- cultures of peace

- fairness, justice, and rights

- the end of patriarchy

- global greening

- the interreligious movement

- words that made a difference

Each manifests the first stirrings of an emerging global consensus of values. We'll take that up shortly. For now, let's examine why each of the emergents listed represents major sea-change values rather than minor shifts.

Cultures of Peace

Belligerence is a learned behavior and can be unlearned. In the first phase of the current sea change, the question of war has been explored as never before. Two ancient concepts framed the theory of a "just war": *jus ad bellum* (the justification for going to war) and *jus in bello* (the justification of behavior *in* war).

Both principles of a just war have been challenged in our time as never before. On the horizon is another extraordinary emergent value, "War No More," the persuasive notion that modern major war has become obsolete. Our own early twenty-first-century period will be remembered as the threshold crossing.

The study of conflict resolution made a significant contribution in this area, advancing undreamed-of technologies for encounter, dialogue, and "getting to Yes." On the horizon are new diplomatic and geopolitical voices urging an end to major war and the first stirrings of the shift from redemptive violence to restorative justice. The prophetic American theologian Walter Wink has written about the fading of the older myth that violence is often the only recourse for the redemption of what has been lost (rights, land, dignity, etc.). He argues that we are entering the province of a new mythic understanding, in which (nonviolent) justice is the only recourse for restoration.

Fairness, Justice, Rights

This century may well be recalled as the period that ended major war; but perhaps an even more significant appellation would be "the century of justice." The great philosopher John Rawls once offered a famous test of the understanding of justice. Imagine that you can change any of the world's social rules or realities, redistributing talent, wealth, power, etc., as you please. But in the morning, when you awaken, you will be someone else. Only one criterion can possibly guide your decisions, Rawls argued—simple fairness is the key. This criterion may be remembered as the signature challenge of the twenty-first century. Or perhaps, it may be recalled as the challenge to which the twentieth century inspired its successor to arise.

Marking the crossing into the twenty-first was the United Nations' promulgation of the first global call for fairness: the eight Millennium Development Goals (MDG), endorsed by the General Assembly and a strong majority of member states in the year 2000. The challenge asked the world community to meet these goals before the end of the century's second decade. While it's now clear that the deadline may not be met—largely because of the global economic crisis—activists dare to hope that the goals themselves are not out of reach. The eight goals are:

- relief of global poverty and hunger

- universal primary education

- gender equity

- child health

- maternal health

- HIV-AIDS alleviation

- ecological sustainability

- global partnerships forged to meet these ends

CHAPTER 6

The End of Patriarchy

I like to imagine Rhett Butler reincarnated in the twenty-first century and meeting his great-great-great-granddaughter. Needless to say, Rhett is brought up short by the sharp contrast between her views and his own on a whole range of intimately intertwined issues, including the role of women, slavery, racism, and justice.

The world has changed, and a reborn Rhett might be among the first to recognize it. The patriarchal assumption persisted from the rise of the hominids through three major sea changes. The challenge and rejection of Rhett's values means that one of the longest lasting of the old thresholds has been breached.

At the 1993 Parliament of the World's Religions, I heard Professor Susannah Heschel make an astonishing connection: "It's not accidental that we call her 'Mother Earth,'" she said, "and then proceed to treat her exactly as we have always treated women." Fortunately, things have changed since then, and we're moving rapidly toward gender equality in ways that might have struck Rhett as scandalous.

Global Greening

Anyone who hasn't noticed the "greening" of the global conversation hasn't been paying attention. Anyone who believes that the planetary value system hasn't greened needs to do more inquiry. But is this really an emergent value or more talk than action?

Recycling is inspiring, but still rather inconsequential. Cutting down one's carbon footprint is far more meaningful, but still limited. Individuals trading carbon usage by paying premiums is good, but simply not enough. But we are seeing a great many committed environmentalists taking the next step, one that involves advancing cultural awareness. As we learn more about the interdependence of the global ecosystem, more complex analysis produces a vast array of new options, from alternative energy, to "smart houses," to better food choices, to improved waste handling. And, of course, the human solution is *quadratic*. I can reflect more deeply on my personal values; I can become more engaged in local, regional, national, and global culture. I can, in short, become more activist at a level that suits my interests and options. I certainly can become more aware of ecoscience and of the variety of socioeconomic implications of the key problems and varieties of proposed solutions.

Cultural evolution is well underway because of popular willingness combined with systemic change. If I want to recycle, I must engage with the recycling system (or lack thereof). Where do I get my energy? How do I recycle it? Do these questions define my energy profile? And how do I diminish my carbon profile? Even asking these questions suggests that a major change is already underway. If I'm asking these questions, I've crossed the threshold.

The Interreligious Movement

For the past twenty years I've been engaged on a fool's errand, or so I've often been told. During that period, I have been active in the global movement for interreligious dialogue and engagement. Those who disparage the effort usually come from one of two very different starting points:

1. Religions differ in their basic premises; only one can be true. Therefore, interreligious engagement can only imperil the faith of the true believer.

2. Religion is the source of all human problems. The sooner we are finished with it, the better. Dialogue only prolongs the inevitable.

Yet the interreligious engagement movement flourishes despite the naysayers. In 1960, virtually no city on Earth had a serious interreligious program. By the year 2000, most of the larger cities did. Something

129

had changed. What's more, by 2008, most of those efforts were yielding programs of social outreach and ecological rescue. Consider, too, the proliferation of global organizations dedicated to interreligious goals: the International Association for Religious Freedom, the World Conference on Religion and Peace, the International Peace Council, the Council for a Parliament of the World's Religions, and the United Religions Initiative.

Words That Make a Difference

The wisest words of an age of transition will be of immense value not only to that age but also to those that follow. The following list is based on two measures: How broad is the vision of the declaration? And how widely was it received? On the basis of these two criteria, I've listed the most formative, thematic, and instructive documents of our time.

Reading these eight extraordinary documents clearly demonstrates the evolution of our twentieth-century focus on the critical issues *and* the development of a shared vocabulary that is helping to shape the emerging global consensus on peacemaking, human rights, and ecological sanity.

People often ask, just what good are conferences and their declarations about how things should be? From our sea-change perspective, they often embody the latest iteration of a maturing idea or value set. The three key precipitating elements of evolutionary thought and action are new visions, new ideas, and new language. Each of the following distinguishing documents of the twentieth century brings all three to bear on the major problems and challenges of our age.

Read the following eight statements (all are available online), and decide whether or not you discern an evolution of vision, ideas, and language.

- *The Universal Declaration of Human Rights* (1948: no peace or progress without human rights): http://www.un.org/en/documents/udhr/

- *The Brandt Report* (1980: international development): http://www.stwr.org/special-features/the-brandt-report.html

- *The Brundtland Report* (1987: environmental problems global in nature; our common human obligation to address them): http://www.undocuments.net/a42r187.htm

- *The Seville Statement on Violence* (1986: violence not part of the human condition; learned and unlearnable behavior): http://portal.unesco.org/education/en/ev.php-URL_ID=3247&URL_DO=DO_TOPIC&URL_SECTION=201.html

- *Towards a Global Ethic: An Initial Declaration* (Parliament of the World's Religions, 1993: ethical principles on which the world's religions can come together): http://www.parliamentofreligions.org/_includes/FCKcontent/File/TowardsAGlobalEthic.pdf

- *A Call to Our Guiding Institutions* (Parliament of the World's Religions, 1999: interreligious outreach to the world's key institutions regarding the critical issues facing the twenty-first century): http://www.parliamentofreligions.org/_includes/FCKcontent/File/CalltoGuidingInstitutions.pdf

- *The Earth Charter* (1987–2000: environmental protection, human rights, equitable development, and peace): http://www.earthcharterinaction.org/content/pages/Read-the-Charter.html

- *The UN Millennium Development Goals* (2000: social justice, gender equity, global partnership): http://www.un.org/millenniumgoals/

VALUES WHOSE TIME HAS COME

No one is quite sure who originated the phrase "Think globally and act locally," although it's been attributed to figures as disparate as Buckminster Fuller and Saul Alinsky. Whatever its provenance, it has endured as

131

perhaps the best known of the slogans of the early years of the current sea change. In one sense it's as true as ever, but in another it requires a basic reimagining. Most of us will never have our hands on the levers of global power or access to world-changing wealth. We are constrained to act locally (while refining our global vision). But the situation has actually changed dramatically.

As a result of the networking power of the Internet, the "new local" can be anywhere in the world. Here's an example. In 2004, my wife and I traveled to Kenya as part of the Globalization for the Common Good initiative. One of the members of the group was Todd Lorentz, a young Canadian very active in the Global Commons movement. As we traveled through an endless string of desperately poor villages, many struggling with the plight of AIDS orphans, Todd decided to act locally, in Kenya, from Alberta, Canada. Today, the One Child's Village program operates a number of schools and clinics that make a very significant local difference with a decidedly global flavor.

None of us has a crystal ball, but the following section suggests themes that are likely to play major roles over the course of the next several years. They are grouped into several clusters that may prove useful as we reflect on what the future may look like.

I. The P, J, S Connection

While the already-emergent values discussed above all have powerful implications for peace, justice, and sustainability, our cultural mindset doesn't fully grasp the fundamental linkage of these three concepts. Peace and nonviolent conflict resolution, human rights and economic and social justice, and ecological sustainability will likely become the guiding principles of international polity and global governance. In many circles, they are already referred to simply as "p, j, and s."

One powerful indicator is the ongoing work of the United Nations and thousands of nongovernmental organizations on the Millennium

Development Goals. These groups are strongly committed to the emerging global consensus. Peace and nonviolent conflict resolution can be achieved in our time. Human rights and social and economic justice are realizable. Ecological sustainability must become an attainable reality.

As the new wave advances, several emergent metavalues will likely come to the fore. These overarching principles will help to shape the interconnection of peace, justice, and sustainability during our sea change. The concept of world community is already coming into common usage. Our guiding myth will no longer be redemptive violence, but restorative justice. We will begin to explore and act on the preferential option for the poor. Harkening to our native brothers and sisters, we will begin to think seven generations ahead.

The interdependent complexity of p, j, and s surfaces in the list of specific goals that follows. In a very real sense, the attainment of any one depends in part on the attainment of the others. Taken together, the following three families of goal principles comprise an emerging global consensus of values that is one of the most salient features of the current sea change.

Peace
- Honesty and integrity in all relations, with other individuals, communities, cultures, and nations

- Human relations characterized by respect, generosity, hospitality, and personal responsibility

- Harmony and equity between the genders

- Freedom from war and violence and terror

- Relief from global, national, and regional political disruptions and dislocations

- Political leaders committed to the local and global commonweal

- Religious and spiritual leaders committed to mutual respect, peace, nonviolence, and cooperation between and among ethnic, racial, cultural, and religious communities

Justice

- Provision of adequate shelter, food, and clean water for all

- Elimination of global poverty

- Reduction of the gap in wealth and status between rich and poor

- Promotion of good health for all

- Provision of equal educational opportunity for all

- Protection and promotion of civil and political rights for all

- Freedom of speech and religious/spiritual belief and practice

- An end to crime and corruption in society

- Protection and promotion of economic and social rights for marginalized groups, especially women, children, and the poor

- Relief from global, national, and regional economic disruptions and dislocations

Sustainability

- A healthy and vibrant Earth

- Respect and attention to the needs of future generations for a sustainable future

- Relief from global, national, and regional ecological and resource disruptions and dislocations

- Sustainable and mutually enhancing human relations with the Earth

- Respect and concern for the rights of other species and the Earth as a whole

- Human production and consumption in harmony with the Earth

- Human population supportable by ecological and social systems

- An end to unsustainable abuse of Earth, ecosystems, and species

II. The Global Common Good

What is the "common good"? If every global cultural advance brings something better to every global citizen, we are on the mark. The first key lies in the realization that something is possible and vital.

How do we search out the very best for the greatest number of people? The ideal of seeking the common good is the direct opposite of the notion of trickle-down economics. Here, the animating notion is that the economic world, like the physical universe, is complex and interdependent. When we apply our benchmarks, our desired outcome should clearly benefit a wide range of social groups. It should make sense with respect to the physical systems of our world. And it should enrich the life of every participating individual. At the same time, the global common good must be approached in a quadratic manner. We need to consider not only its scientific and social-scientific dimensions, but its religious, political, and cultural facets as well. And our approach has to be grounded in personal experience, in the spiritual and artistic values that provide our deepest insights and strengths.

The global common good must be understood in the context of (at least) the following criteria.

CHAPTER 6

Globalization from the Bottom Up

The process of globalization can be viewed from at least two contrasting perspectives. As a top-down phenomenon, it is often accompanied by a number of disturbing phenomena, including

- destructive effects on local economies,

- cultural homogenization with a Northern flavor, and

- a corresponding felt threat to social, political, economic, and cultural identity in many regions of the world.

Top-down globalization—as is evident in the astonishing range and complexity of current worldwide tensions—lends credibility to the otherwise questionable notion of an impending clash of civilizations.

On the other hand, considerable evidence suggests that a counter-vailing phenomenon is underway: globalization from the bottom up. It is manifest in the emerging global consensus of values with respect to peace, social and economic justice, gender equity, human rights, and ecological sustainability—a consensus that is observable among activists to be sure, but increasingly evident in significant segments of the larger world population.

All over the developing world, nongovernmental groups, individual activists, and intergovernmental agencies are working to create new options for the poor and a wide range of alternatives to Northern economic and cultural domination. Empowered by Internet-based communications, the new globalization shares resources and problem-solving techniques and creates new partnerships between individuals and groups that can work closely together without frequent and costly face-to-face meetings.

For the last several years, two global gatherings have drawn the global line. One at Davos, Switzerland, has drawn together the movers and shakers of the global financial game. The other, at Puerto Allegre, Brazil, has assembled a counterassembly focused on issues of poverty, justice, and human rights. The growing dialogical interaction between the two summits (usually held at the same time) is one of the most promising signs of what is to come.

Global Citizenship: Youth and the Future

Do we want the best and brightest of our children to belong to the future instead of the past? If so, we want to invite our children to seek out the widest possible experiences. A number of college and graduate programs offer wide-ranging experiences for students: semesters abroad; four-year programs set in several different cultural and linguistic settings; broad-based political, cultural, and activist opportunities.

But the real question is straightforward: would you rather be a citizen of the United States or a citizen of the world? The answer we hear from growing numbers of young cosmopolitans is, "How can I possibly be a citizen of the United States without being first a citizen of the world?"

Global Commons: The Ecumene

The earth, air, oceans, airwaves, and even the Internet are the modern global commons, comparable to the village commons and surrounds where long ago sheep were pastured, children played, and gardens were planted. What had long been regarded as a basic right of "the people" began to be eroded by the process of "enclosure," as first kings and then modern nation-states claimed the commons for their own use.

Now a new virtual community is taking shape. Its goal is the definition, declaration, and defense of the commons. While the concept is still largely unfamiliar even to educated audiences, watch for it. It's just crossing the horizon.

Global Governance

Decades ago, considerable support existed for the idea of a single world government. We no longer seek that end. Rather, we are fascinated with the possibilities of global *governance*.

We have realized that the critical problems that face the global community are interdependent. There is no "local air," no "local water," no "local land." The interdependence of all these systems gives rise to the global ecosystem. And the only way to regulate such a complex interdependent whole is through global governance.

III. Restoring the *Oikos*

The modern age violated the *oikos*, the Earth household. Over time, it broke several covenants with the home world. Now, however, their restoration no longer seems out of reach. It's important to realize the interdependent complexity of ecology, economy, and ecumenism. Each of the aspects of the long-neglected *oikos* will find its expression in the advancing new wave.

Ecology: The Principles of the Earth Home

Four decades ago, the first Earth Day was celebrated in the United States. Quickly, the phenomenon spread around the country and around the world. Then, somehow, it seemed to fade. Now a growing global ecological consciousness has reemerged. Strike up a conversation with a younger person. How are his or her values different from yours today or, at least, from your "starter kit" of socioeconomic values? Need any further demonstration of cultural evolution? If so, now imagine a conversation with your own grandparents.

We encountered ecological sustainability among the already-emergent values, but a deeper commitment seems likely to be on the way. Imagine a culture in which the first law of daily interaction with energy, waste, and the environment, is "Do no harm" or "Leave no trace." The fact that we no longer find such a concept inconceivable is the first indication that it might be attainable.

Economy: The Law of the Earth Family

That an implosion of the long-dominant capitalist system was required to open the door to long-developing alternative models is ironic. From the creation of new ways of measuring wealth, costs, and profits, to the development of a new global currency, to the long-neglected defense of the global commons, new economic models are emerging.

The challenge to the destructive effect of unrestricted market capitalism could not be clearer. And the current global economic crisis, whose effects will be felt for decades, may ironically provide the opening to serious consideration of alternatives.

Clearly, as Adam Smith realized in his later years, the "engine of human acquisitiveness" becomes, in time, a juggernaut of untamed greed. At least it's no longer a hidden reality.

The New Ecumenism

Note that two of the world-changing documents listed above were produced by the Parliament of the World's Religions. As a founding trustee who served for several years as global director of that organization, I confess a strong bias. But it's hard to gainsay the significance of the Parliament and the other global interreligious movements. In our age, more people have come to know more about more other religions and cultures than has ever been the case. One might even argue that knowing so much about the other diminishes the role of the stranger and makes the enclave-building task of the fundamentalist immeasurably more difficult.

Professor Hans Küng, the pioneer of the international effort toward a global ethic, argues that the key to world peace lies in interreligious mutuality. I agree.

While the interreligious movement was one of our already emergents, true ecumenism remains just out of reach. Too much ignorance fuels too much antipathy. But reasons for hope abound.

The signs of an almost unparalleled cultural value shift are evident on all sides. And, gradually, as our awareness of cultural anomalies becomes more acute, our questions are getting better as well.

Still, it's all too evident that the transformation is not unopposed. In the next chapter, we'll discover how cultural change can generate confusion, identity crisis, and threats to the structures of power. The tumult that ensues from these disturbances presents the greatest threat to the cultural-evolutionary leap we are contemplating.

Next we began to sail up the narrow strait lamenting. For on the one hand lay Scylla, and on the other mighty Charybdis in terrible wise sucked down the salt water.

—Homer, *The Odyssey*

The edge of the whirl was represented by a broad belt of gleaming spray; but no particle of this slipped into the mouth of the terrific funnel, whose interior, as far as the eye could fathom it, was a smooth, shining, and jet-black wall of water . . . speeding dizzily round and round with a swaying and sweltering motion, and sending forth to the winds an appalling voice, half shriek, half roar, such as not even the mighty cataract of Niagara ever lifts up in its agony to Heaven. . . . "This," said I at length, to the old man— "this can be nothing else than the great whirlpool of the Maelstrom."

—Edgar Allan Poe, "A Descent into the Maelstrom"

7

Maelstrom

The literature of the sea is replete with tales of turbulent whirlpools whose violent spin and powerful suction carry unwary travelers to their doom. Perhaps the most famous of the real vortices is Norway's Lofoten Maelstrom, an occasional tidal disturbance so powerful that its name has become a generic term for a particularly violent whirlpool. The Lofoten was the inspiration for Edgar Allan Poe's "A Descent Into the Maelstrom." In Poe's account, two fishermen are lost but a third returns, as if reborn, to tell a story no one will believe. A recurrent theme in tales of this sort is that one either perishes in the vortex or rides it out and is somehow flung miraculously to safety. Maelstrom narratives draw on several other shared themes: terror, loss of control, swirling confusion and disorientation, death and rebirth. But the most essential character of whirlpools lies in the fact that each is born from the convergence of opposing forces.

The Lofoten Maelstrom offers the best metaphor for our purposes. The maelstrom arises as a result of a dramatic discontinuity in the ocean floor that disturbs the tidal flow, allowing *a rising tide to begin its inflow well before the preceding tide has ebbed*. The consequence, of course, is a confusion of flows, generating a rotary chaos that can escalate dramatically and very rapidly.

Whirlpools, vortices, and maelstroms are all variations on a single, theme: the *eddy*. As a turbulent gyre emerging from the interference of two or more waves, currents, or tides, the eddy makes an apt metaphor for an anti-evolutionary counterflow. The tide of cultural evolution may be felt long before the failing older value wave has subsided. As a consequence, countless eddies emerge—whirlpools of perplexity and powerlessness. As a temporary but potentially violent pattern of resistance forming at the confluence of the older and newer waves, the cultural eddy is one of the most common and most misunderstood dynamics of human social evolution.

ENTERING THE WHIRLPOOL

In the usual course of events, resistance to change takes form in a stubborn but relatively benign attachment to familiar ways. But when the change is pronounced, more striking forms of reaction and resistance emerge. When the threatened social transformation seems as dramatic and far reaching as it does in our time, the opposition can lose touch with older values like tolerance and civility and become rootless, angry, and dangerous.

In a period of sea change, a culture is always taken aback by the increasing influence of new ideas and values. In the transition phase, older *ideas* (e.g., the notion that the Earth is the center of the universe) give way more graciously than do older *values* and *cultural patterns* (e.g., the superiority of the male). In each case, however, resistance occurs. Our ideas, values, and cultural behavior patterns have a quality akin to physical inertia (resistance to change in motion). When they are challenged, the interruption of their flow generates counterenergies, and eddies can form.

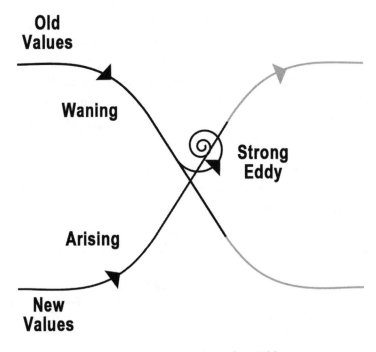

Figure 7.1. Formation of an Eddy

As tempting as it is to see disturbing cultural phenomena, ranging from road rage to identity politics and terrorism, as indications of the likely future course of the world, many of the signature problems of our age need to be understood instead as *phenomena of the crossing*. These are *not* manifestations of the declining older wave or unfortunate features of the newer wave. They are temporary but dangerous reactive counter-flows—eddies—that can slow but not stem the new tide. The dictionary definition underscores the aptness of the metaphor: 1 a movement in a stream of air, water, or other fluid in which the current doubles back on itself causing a miniature whirlwind or whirlpool; 2 a deviation from or disturbance in the main trend of thought, life, etc., esp. one that is relatively unimportant in the longer term.

When the rhythm of a smoothly flowing stream is disturbed, eddies can emerge, temporary whirlpools that roil the water in their immediate vicinity without really affecting the prevailing flow. The analogy works. In a time of major evolutionary cultural change, when prevailing patterns are challenged and disrupted, individuals and groups can be caught up in an outflow of the familiar and inflow of the new. If the perturbation affects a sufficient number of persons or power centers, a major eddy can form. In culture, as in nature, no change exists without resistance. Eddies emerge, persist, and dissipate in the course of cultural transitions of every sort. However, the degree of cultural opposition to change increases in direct proportion to the cultural disruption produced by a values shift. Uncertainty, insecurity, alienation, identity crisis, humiliation, and power anxiety determine the force of a cultural whirlpool. Its manifestations may range from minor turbulence and patterns of stubborn refusal to extremely dangerous and potentially violent backwash. Agents of change need to understand what happens when an eddy of cultural resistance becomes a violent reactionary maelstrom.

Counterflow

Plus ça change, plus c'est la même chose. The more things change, the more they stay the same. That familiar witticism was first penned in nineteenth-century France by journalist Alphonse Karr as a somewhat cynical dismissal of the notion that human culture might evolve and improve. Clearly, Karr was not a fan of cultural evolution. His world-weary point, though, is that the more things change, the more determinedly some people try to hang on to older ways. The more the change confuses them, challenges their sense of identity, or diminishes their power, the more they'll fight back in an effort to keep things "the same."

Each sea change is shaped by remembrances of the past and visions of the future. As is the case with sight of every sort, acuity is essential. If my vision of the past is a sort of wistful myopia, my focus on the future will likely be similarly impaired.

The tension inherent in the wave crossing from modernity to the emerging twenty-first-century ethos is evident in several key *currents of change*:

- new scientific understandings,

- the Internet and other modes of global communication,

- increasingly informed concern about planetary social and ecological realities,

- globally integrated networks of committed activists for peace, justice, sustainability, etc., and

- new interreligious and intercultural movements for a better world.

At the same time, one can also discern some fundamental *currents of resistance*:

- cultural habit patterns,

- institutional inertia,

- ingrained value complexes,

- personal and group identity structures, and

- established centers of cultural, political, economic, and social power.

Most students of culture understand not only the energy of the currents of change but also the inertial power of the currents of resistance. If the only things to consider were the two waves, the analysis of a sea change would be complex but fairly straightforward. But something more is at work.

On every side in our young century, disturbing new configurations of cultural values, attitudes, and behaviors are emerging that do not seem to belong to either wave complex. The list is familiar, from epidemic bad manners to aggressive fundamentalism and the terrifying specter of identity violence. These emergent patterns seem at first to be reversions to some earlier (modern or even premodern) cultural value set, but the reality is not so simple. Fundamentalism, for example, is decidedly *not* a return to "old-time religion," though it often masquerades as such. Rather, it is a phenomenon of the twentieth century. As Karen Armstrong puts it in her extraordinary work *The Battle for God* (which addresses Jewish, Christian, and Muslim fundamentalism), "There have always been people, in every age and in each tradition, who have fought the modernity of their day. But the fundamentalism that we shall be considering is an essentially twentieth-century movement."[1]

So it is with each of the disturbing cultural patterns that will be examined in this chapter. None belong to the incoming culture wave; in fact, each is strongly resistant to most or all of the new values. Even more curiously, none are really part of the older wave, although professed allegiance to "traditional values" is a familiar element of the rhetoric of resistance. For example, patriarchal backlash and the alarming recent rise in violence toward women are phenomena of our own time, not a return to earlier rhythms. Similarly, twentieth- and twenty-first-century fundamentalism, antiscience, neoimperialism, terrorism, and other countercurrents are *emergent* forms, born of turbulence.

From the point of crossing, the voyager (whether enthusiastic or reluctant) gazes in two directions: back along the path of the subsiding culture wave and ahead along the unrealized course of the advancing swell. The clearer my view of the past and my vision of the future, the less likely it is that I will be pulled into an eddy of resistance to cultural evolution.

Let's take a brief look at two characteristically American cultural eddies. The first is a relatively new force in early twenty-first-century politics. The second has been churning away in conservative Christian communities for over eighty years but has grown dramatically in the last three decades.

THE RED BLUES

Aficionados of the U.S. political scene acquired a new hobby at the beginning of the twenty-first century: dividing the map of the country into red and blue zones. We began to hear that America was polarized as never before, statistically split down the middle between liberal "blues" and conservative "reds." The former are identified with relatively progressive social, fiscal, domestic, and foreign policies. The latter are supposedly tied to a conservative interpretation of Christianity and narrowly defined moral values, in particular, opposition to abortion and gay marriage.

In reality, most major regions of the country are politically diverse, more purple than red or blue. In recent years, a strong blue shift has taken place. Moreover, clearly not all red voters are extreme cultural conservatives or born-again Christians. Nevertheless, the talk of polarization is not entirely fanciful, and the red-blue dichotomy will likely be with us for some time to come. (Interestingly, the new coding—apparently born in a network television graphics studio during the presidential campaign of 2000—involved the unwitting reversal of the venerable British tradition that assigned the color blue to conservative Tories and red to democrats, Whigs, liberals, and finally, socialists.)

Since the 1970s, America does seem to have experienced a dramatic increase in red or retro cultural and electoral energy. If true, that development poses a clear challenge to the sea-change thesis. While progressive political values have grown in influence in recent years, who's to say that rightward political movement is not the *real* wave of the future? The global economic crisis of 2008 clearly exacerbated that tendency in Europe, Africa, and elsewhere. If, in fact, we're living at the leading edge of a major, positive cultural evolutionary wave, what is the source of the strong manifestations of reactionary energy in so many dimensions of American life?

Chapter 3 introduced the three benchmarks of genuine cultural evolution: an increase in creative complexity, growing awareness of interdependence, and the rise of integral approaches to knowing. You'd have to be culturally blind to deny these things are happening. More to the point, consider these examples of benchmark factors: ecology, pluralism, and a broadening of the spiritual search. If people are embracing such values worldwide, it signifies a huge change in society. Not surprisingly, pockets of opposition have formed in response.

Consider the following list of statistically high-scoring values among red voters in the United States. Every item in some way embodies a negative reaction to the decline of older cultural assumptions and a strong stance against rising newer ones. Some deny cultural complexity and interdependence. Others reject the integration of different areas of knowledge. Most tellingly, each represents a point of view that is actually in decline—in the United States and around the world. (Cf. John Sperling, *The Great Divide: Retro v. Metro America*, and Stanley Greenberg, *The Two Americas*.)[2]

- American values and culture bestride the world.

- Exclusivism and fundamentalism are the proper religious attitudes.

- Separation of church and state is a dangerous myth.

- Religion trumps science.

- The theory of evolution is a destructive hoax.

- Morality primarily concerns sexual behavior.

- Homosexuality is a violation of God's law.

- Women's essential role is in the home.

- Gun control is a violation of a founding American liberty.

- American foreign policy should be based on unilateralism, not multilateralism.

- Multiculturalism and diversity should be strongly resisted.

- Poverty is a failure of self-sufficiency.

- The theory of global warming is unfounded.

- Ecological issues should not be legislated.

If we're moving toward a more complex and integrated understanding of our interdependent world, how do we account for the regional reddening of America and the supposed return to traditional values that some pundits see as the most formidable political current of our age? Not surprisingly, the answer lies in a deeper understanding of counterevolutionary eddies.

The culture shock that produces the red/retro eddy is fed, of course, by visions of past and future. However, in this case, the adherents gaze fondly into a misremembered past and stare horrified into a misunderstood future. The media rantings of reactionary demagogues nurture this false hindsight.

One who has only sepia-tinged memories of the past as a better time than the present might understandably feel horror at an imagined future. Some perhaps remember the 1950s in America as a time of tranquil rectitude and family values, but don't recall the murder of fourteen-year-old Emmett Till in Money, Mississippi. Others remember the forty-four-inch fins on designer Harley Earl's 1956 Cadillac Eldorado Seville, but don't really see any connection between the consumer culture of that decade and the array of critical issues that face the world today. Most of us certainly recall the advent of "the pill," but too many forget the systematic oppression of women that was even then building toward a cultural

151

crisis. We may remember Dwight Eisenhower's eight-year presidency as a time of cultural clarity and American pride, and yet somehow all but forget the collective darkness of the McCarthy period.

At the same time, some may actually dread the coming of a future that will bring the demise of American Judeo-Christian values, the destruction of the family, and a cosmopolitan tyranny that will erode every last value and destroy the very idea of liberty. And so they begin to yield to the pull of the eddy and to experience its calming disconnect from an intolerable reality.

Now let's turn from politics to religion, the latter inviting even more hysterical reactions than the former.

OF MONKEYS AND MEN

When Charles Darwin published *The Descent of Man* in 1871, the religious hue and cry was moderate. One eminent Victorian, the wife of the Bishop of London, is famously reported to have said, "I certainly hope that Mr. Darwin will not be proven right; but if he should be, I hope that it will not become widely known." Churchmen and socialites were more baffled than alarmed by the suggestion that the nearest relatives of human beings were the hairier primates, the apes. For the most part, however, the response was less visceral than intellectual. Darwin's evolutionary schema had, of course, already been published eleven years earlier in *On the Origin of Species*. *The Descent* now added humans to the list of species that owed their biological form to the process of random mutation and natural selection. Two words in the preceding sentence, however, encapsulate the story of the powerful anti-Darwinian reaction of the early twentieth century: *random* and *natural*.

The creationist movement that emerged in the early 1920s in America took angry exception to the notion that the appearance of humans on planet Earth was a random or a natural event. In this view, Darwinian evolution was one of three "great errors" that energized the modern Christian fundamentalist venture. The second was the growth (in Germany in particular) of "higher criticism"—the literary analysis and exegesis of Jewish and Christian scripture. The last was the Social Gospel movement—a liberal development in American Protestantism that sought to address poverty, social injustice, and human hopelessness. Today, of course, the anti-evolution movement is one of the signature eddies resisting the twenty-first-century sea change; and it remains closely allied to scriptural literalism and social conservatism.

This book is based on the concept of cultural evolution, which presumes the reality of biological evolution, supported by overwhelming scientific consensus. One has to wonder about the real sources of the long and increasingly bitter hostility to evolutionary theory. To answer that question, we need to supply some historical context.

In 1925, the famous Scopes trial marked the first major public appearance of the fundamentalist phenomenon. A reaction against modernism in theology and contemporary life, fundamentalism began to define itself in the early years of the century. It was strongly rooted in a "back to the Bible" literalism and a deeply conservative view of human society. From its very early days, American fundamentalism saw the theory of evolution as the most insidious of all the misguided notions inflaming the modern world.

To deny the scientific evidence supporting *some* form of biological evolution is vastly more difficult today than it was in 1925 at the time of the celebrated trial. Yet the opposition has grown from a largely Southern rural base to a nationwide subculture that celebrates an anti-evolution and antiscience view of the world. As one popular slogan has it, "I'm more concerned about the Rock of Ages than the age of rocks."

What do creationists fear? And how did evolution become a political issue—so significant that a president of the United States could actually declare that "the jury is out" on biological evolution? Creationism and the later intelligent-design movement are rooted in the belief that the random character of evolution contradicts the belief in a creator God and a divinely decreed moral order. A moral decline, therefore, is seen as a direct effect of the widespread acceptance of the "random" and "natural" assumptions of evolutionary theory. The erosion of the family (read "liberation of women") and the increase in abortions, homosexuality, drug use, violence, etc., can all be laid at Mr. Darwin's door.

Again, imaginings of an Eden-like past and a hellish future shape the anti-evolution movement. Its proponents envision a future of human-centered indulgence and indiscipline. A literal reading of the Bible that seems to support the "young Earth" notion embraced by most anti-evolutionists shapes the view of the past. If scripture attests to a world less than one hundred centuries old, the extravagant claims of the Darwinians must be rejected. The Earth is at most ten thousand years old, hardly 4.5 billion.

And here's the real reason why this eddy is swirling so rapidly: it's a reaction against science. Science represents a direct challenge to the hegemony of scripture as the definitive criterion for judgments about reality. In the early twentieth century, an attack on evolution seemed the most effective strategy for a major assault on science. Easy to caricature and burdened with many unresolved internal controversies, Darwinian theory was regarded as open to misinterpretation and mockery. Thus the "evolution wars" began; and so they continue to this day.

Those who fear the rise of human reason (i.e., science) as a threat to religious revelation have embraced pseudoscientific arguments of the creationists and intelligent design campaigners. Now two eddies are in play: fundamentalism and antiscience.

THE WHIRLPOOL CATALOGUE

Why are people drawn into eddies? Given that the eddy is a metaphor for dizzying cultural dislocation, who would want to be pulled into its vertiginous waters?

We need to recognize that there are at least three distinct categories of eddy, each rooted in one of three interrelated aspects of human experience and behavior: culture, identity, and power. All three types represent reaction patterns rather than waves of the future. This distinction is particularly important since much of the pessimism of the naysayers results from a misunderstanding of the significance of eddies in relation to evolutionary advance. It's easy to misperceive an eddy as a part of the so-called new wave and therefore resist the culture shift. As we examine the three types of eddies, we recognize how truly reactionary they are.

Cultural Confusion

Eddies of this sort are patterns of resistance to changing life conditions and altered behavioral expectations. When behavioral standards break down and people are befuddled by the world around them, eddies start to form. Those caught in the cultural-confusion eddy stop conforming and start wandering; they become apathetic, fall into an existential funk, or embrace amorality. These patterns of emergent disconnection tend to be among the milder eddies, though they fuel the others. Most of the naysayers are victims of some combination of cultural confusion and identity crisis, our next eddy type.

Those who are convinced that ours is an age of moral decay and devolution often complain of fading social niceties, changing definitions of "truth," aimless youth, or the collapse of the standards "we were raised with." What they're really saying is they don't *get it* (the cultural shift). Consider a simple example. The erosion of the patriarchal social system undercuts the entire structure of Western etiquette. When gender roles are thrown into confusion, how are men and women to know the appropriate modes of interaction?

Earlier I identified initial symptoms of the modern value wave's ebb, from the breakdown of traditional civility to a bored lack of interest in the world, and from postmodern relativism to religious and political thralldom. Each of these phenomena is an attempted escape from bewildering cultural confusion. When the sociocultural order suddenly becomes too complex or too agitated, disengagement can take many forms. Cults, conspiracy theories, and deconstructive relativism are among the least socially troublesome; abject submission to charismatic leadership is one of the most perilous. While eddies in this first category tend to produce less direct social dislocation, they nevertheless supply the more dangerous types of eddy with the energy of identity crisis.

Identity Crisis

Alienation is a powerful life-changer. Karl Marx saw it as the catalyst of the downfall of the bourgeois economic and social orders. In our own time, it has become a major wellspring of terrorism. The sense of isolation, of loss of belonging, can produce a psychological crisis in which the individual or group feels cut off not only from the prevailing social order, but also from the real world. While the great majority of people and communities can weather challenges to prevailing assumptions without pathological alienation, occasionally a critical threshold is crossed.

In our own age, many find the world-shrinking forces of globalization unbearably threatening to personal, family, religious, or cultural identity. In his remarkable book *In the Name of Identity: Violence and the Need to Belong*, Amin Maalouf offers a useful insight: "To tell the truth, if we assert our differences so fiercely, it is precisely because we are less and less different from one another."[3]

In a globalizing world, the identity-challenged usually attempt to redefine themselves over and against other groups. Too often the effort yields to the dangerous temptation to identify oneself in terms of the perceived vices of the other, rather than in terms of one's own virtues or aspirations. Thus, we encounter the familiar formula, "Thank God I'm not . . . [a Serb, a Croat, a Jew, a Muslim, white, Christian, black, a woman . . . the other]."

Extremists bask in the eddy of identity crisis. The phenomenon of religious fundamentalism—an extreme modern intensification of centuries-old religious exclusivism—is similarly bound up with perceived threats to religious and social identity. Inevitably, we arrive at the new global menace of terrorism. As Jessica Stern has shown, when the identity of the group is undermined by alienation, humiliation, loss of status or territory, etc., retributive violence distinguishes the actor from the other.[4] Revenge seems to clarify selfhood. Terrorism in the name of God or tribe begins in a crisis of group identity.

Threatened Power

The third category (threats to power) includes the most intense systemic eddies, emerging from disturbances in the authority grid of the older order. Unrestrained greed, rampant corruption, new patterns of regional and global imperialism, and a new breed of twenty-first-century "illiberal democracies" and tyrannies are all patterns of resistance to cultural evolution. Naysayers tend to see these adverse phenomena as evidence that culture only devolves and never really advances. In fact, eddies are evidence of cultural advance, but the turmoil they create easily obscures that critical fact. The clash between older and newer values produces a great deal of dramatic upheaval.

Power elites are threatened by any challenge to their animating assumptions; and when that happens, they don't react well. Consider the sixteenth century, the epicenter of the sea change that saw the emergence of the three Rs—Renaissance, Reformation, and (Scientific) Revolution. All three dimensions of that era's transformation posed direct threats to the hegemony of the church. It responded by bringing extreme religious, and politico-economic pressures to bear on changing European culture. Hindsight tells us that the outcome—the dawning of the modern age—was virtually inevitable, but Rome saw no handwriting on its walls.

Eddies in this category differ significantly from those of the other two. Challenges to wealth and power generate cynical self-interest rather than concern over the blurring of one's worldview. The response is most often deliberate rather than reflexive and, therefore, more treacherous.

FOUR DEADLY SPINS

In a sea change, new swirls of resistance arise and dissipate ceaselessly. Most are relatively harmless. Some pose more serious threats to the disoriented. Still others are powerful enough to generate widespread cultural turbulence, entrapping those who stray within reach. Of these more virulent surges, the following four are particularly troubling:

- fundamentalism

- fascism

- greed

- hegemony

The first two, fundamentalism and fascism, are ideological, affecting large numbers of people. Identity crisis makes them possible, cultural illusion shapes them, and they serve the power elites. Philosopher Terry Eagleton offers a useful insight: "What persuades men and women to mistake each other from time to time for gods or vermin is ideology."[5] Ideology almost always confuses the fictive with the actual: "Don't bother me with facts; my mind's made up."

The latter two, greed and hegemony, are oligarchical, deliberate creations of power elites. These eddies facilitate exploitation of the many in order to secure the wealth and power of the few. The oligarchies, of course, could never flourish without the ideologies. Fundamentalism and fascism are havens for naysayers of the Unexamined Life and Militant varieties (cf. fig. 1.2). More deceptive resisters—the Buccaneers and Hegemons—manipulate the religious and political fringes for their own advantage. In *What's the Matter With Kansas*, Thomas Frank asked why, in the early twenty-first century, people in America's red heartland consistently voted against their own best interests. The answer was straightforward: they were swept up in a narrative that substituted fallacious accounts of "the invisible hand of the free-market" and "a besieged but strong America" for rational analysis of economic and political realities.[6]

The Ideologies

The Fundamentalist Enclave

Fundamentalism animates several powerful resistance spins. It is the most influential of all modern counterflows. Its powerful centripetal force breeds tightly knit enclaves and kinship structures. Ironically, this tendency enhances the movement's ability to propagate through the ranks of society's disaffected.

Born in the early twentieth century, American Christian fundamentalism emerged from age-old religious exclusivism, the belief that the truth of one's own religion demanded the falsity of all others. As the century progressed, tolerant disdain for other religions developed into widespread hostility, with a new scriptural literalism as the catalyst.

Clearly, the fundamentalist rejects the prevailing cultural flow and resists the decay of so-called traditional values. For many adherents, the driving force is not so much antimodern as it is antiprogressive. As we've seen, the movement in its earliest days saw itself as the last line of resistance to three late-modern evils: the preachers of the Social Gospel movement, the historical critics with their more nuanced reading of scripture, and those who would teach the anti-Gospel of evolution in America's schools. Fundamentalist antipathy to the progressive agenda continues today.

As the battle against evolution makes all too apparent, fundamentalism suffers from a central misunderstanding of the symbolic character of religious expression. Karen Armstrong, in *The Battle for God*, describes two essential modes of human understanding, *mythos* and *logos*.

> Myth was not concerned with practical matters, but with meaning. Unless we find significance in our lives, we mortal men and women fall very easily into despair. . . . [Myth] was also rooted in what we would call the unconscious mind. The various mythological stories, which were not intended to be taken literally, were an ancient form of psychology. . . .
>
> Logos was equally important. Logos was the rational, pragmatic, and scientific thought that enabled men and women to function well in the world. . . . Unlike myth, logos must relate exactly to facts and correspond to external realities.[7]

When religion turns to the dark side, it is often empowered by what Armstrong terms the "mythos-logos error." As the persuasive power of science has grown, desperate religious literalists have tried to transpose the two modalities. Timeless wisdom stories are substituted for modern scientific inquiry; scriptural narrative becomes a reliable source of historical and scientific fact, and real science is dismissed as an elitist tribal tale. Tragically, mythic tales of injustice and even martyrdom at the hands of "the others" grow into unquestioned truths demanding vengeance.

The Cult of Fascism

Like fundamentalism, fascism defines itself in part as a struggle against decadence, but it differs from the former in that it does not seek a return to a real or imagined older order. Fundamentalism arises from threatened exclusivism, fascism from affronted nationalism. The former seeks a return to an imagined time of undisputed theocracy. The latter longs for a new order, a fulfillment of national or racial destiny. The two have usually seemed antithetical. Historical fascism has tended to reject religious orthodoxy, although it has often sought temporary compromise. Hitler, for example, was committed to the eradication of Christianity in the Reich. Nevertheless, fascism and fundamentalism share a number of traits:

- mythos-logos confusion

- cultic preoccupation with tradition

- charismatic leadership

- politics of alienation and populist resentment

- corporatist communal organization

- authoritarian internal structure

- hostility to other religious or political forms

- inherent aggression: redemptive violence

Born in post–World World War I Europe, modern fascism was an autocratic movement dedicated to the exaltation of a nation (and usually a single race) over the individual. Over time, however, it proved surprisingly chameleonic in its adaptation to its cultural, political, and even religious surroundings. After its near triumph and final eclipse in the Second World War, neofascist groups arose in several regions of the world. At the same time, fundamentalist movements were emerging from obscurity in a number of religions (including, of course, Judaism, Christianity, Islam, and Hinduism). Several of these dogmatic creations gradually became so strongly identified with nationalist and/or racialist tenets and so wedded to authoritarian forms that real fundamentalist-fascist hybridization is not uncommon in extremist circles today. The Christian or Muslim religio-fascist, for example, envisions a world in which individualism has faded, degeneracy has been ruthlessly eliminated, discipline is absolute, and the state is the embodiment of the one Truth.

What follows is a brief survey of several of the most powerful offspring of ideological fundamentalism and fascism. "Parent" and "child" eddies alike contribute to the malaise of religious and political troubles in the early twenty-first century. Each interferes with the sea change crossing by providing a steady stream of faith-based or populist themes and abundant willing recruits for manipulation by the oligarchies.

Dominionism

The dominionist is a theocrat, seeking control by a single religious community over local, regional, or national government. Dominionism took several forms in the second half of the twentieth century, including Islamism, Christianism, and Hindutva ("Hinduness"). While dominionist ideology is rooted in religious fundamentalism, its political agenda is usually fascist.

Antiscientism

The dominionist agenda finds a powerful ally in the growing movement of opposition to science as the most important expression of human logos. The antiscience eddy has many manifestations, although the battle against evolution is the most prominent—particularly in its latest incarnation as the crusade for teaching intelligent design in schools. In the United States, fundamentalist antiscience is well served by the dominionist Christian homeschooling movement as well as by several well-funded Christian colleges and think tanks.

Identity Extremism

Defining oneself against the other is almost certainly primeval in origin, but it underlies some of the most noxious social maladies of our time. Racism, nationalism, ethnic hatred (Holocaust denial), religious and political intolerance, sexism, classism, and homophobia all stem from identity insecurity. Fascism itself is more deeply grounded here rather than in economic doctrine or civic theory. Religion, however, has long been the greatest legitimizer of identity extremism.

Violence in the Name of "Ism"

One of the most regrettable signature eddies of the early twenty-first century is global terrorism. While it has strong fascist political overtones, it is clearly rooted in fundamentalism and illustrates the destructive interplay of the parent eddy and its offspins. In the cycle of religious violence, for instance, the encounter with radically different religious identities generates cultural confusion and identity crisis. The fundamentalist demagogue is in his element, offering pseudoreligious redefinitions of self and other. Wealth and power oligarchies manipulate the entire process. The result is all but inevitable: holy violence, terror in the name of God, and the beginning of a vicious cycle.

Violence in the name of the tribe (the nation–state) gives fascism its terrifying power. It owes its origins, however, to the cycle that makes violence seem an appropriate outlet for identity angst.

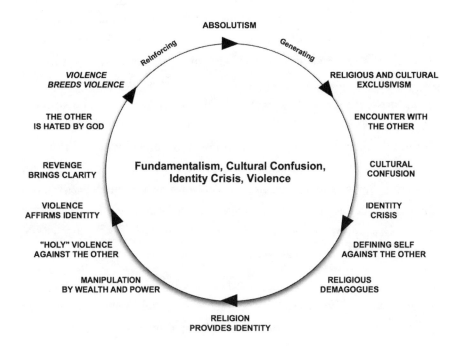

Figure 7.2. Fundamentalism, Cultural Confusion, Identity Crisis, Violence

Figure 7.2 illustrates the Absolutism–Identity Crisis–Violence cycle. It also shows how a particular eddy, in this case, fundamentalism, can generate numerous offspins that combine to create a major cultural crisis.

I noted above that the four deadly spins were of two types, ideological and oligarchical. We've examined the two ideological spins. Now we turn to the latter.

Oligarchies

Globalizing Greed

To author and columnist Thomas Friedman, nothing could be clearer. Globalization is here to stay; one might as well resist the morning sunrise as rail against the new global economy. What's more, Friedman steadily insists, it's basically "all good" rather than all greed. There are losers, of course, but globalization will lift the floor under poverty and empower developing nations. If cultural diversity is lost, a new global convergence will more than make up for it.

That's the cheerleader's view of globalization from the top down— the steady Americanization of planetary economics and popular culture. In fact, however, speculative "casino capitalism" and the global economic crisis that erupted in 2008 are some of unchecked globalization's profoundly damaging consequences. The Buccaneers who led the way through the 1990s to the summit of globalizing greed were intent on extracting every last drop of profit from an overburdened Earth and a superheated economy before the crisis arrived. At every turn, they relied on the ideological eddies (fundamentalism and fascism) to distract the public from power elite agendas.

The Neoliberal Vision

A term seldom heard in the United States is perhaps the most common global epithet for the doctrine of unregulated profit seeking in a global free market. *Neoliberalism* is the modern incarnation of laissez-faire economics as interpreted by the Chicago School, Milton Friedman, Ronald Reagan, and Margaret Thatcher. Its ruthless, value-free policies are best summed up in the largely discredited phrase, "trickle-down," and in Thatcher's famous TINA (there is no alternative).

Neoliberalism embraces the rule of the global market, but it also demands secure access to particular markets. That often requires the use of coercive power, including economic sanctions and the threat or reality of military action.

Banditry: Outlaw Corruption
Corruption, of course, afflicts everyone, but it burdens the poor most of all. Corruption condemns millions to unrelieved poverty and hunger and contributes to socioeconomic and political disorder. It diminishes democracy and cripples private sector ethics. The manipulation of global markets, trade, and banking in the name of individual and corporate profit has brought the world to the brink of the abyss in the first decade of the twenty-first century. Worse still, economic depredation and ecological degradation are intimately intertwined.

Ecocide: Earth Predation
Dormant for years after World War II, environmental awareness was reborn in the turbulent sixties. The next several decades produced new models of sustainability and unprecedented planetary activism. But backlash soon set in.

Globalizing greed manifests itself in many ways: the desperate race to extract oil and other resources from wilderness areas, the resistance to conservation and preservation efforts, and the denial of global climate change. In the face of an emerging global consensus demanding ecological sustainability and virtuous economic practices, these eddies continue to spin.

CHAPTER 7

Hegemony

The increasing likelihood of a major alteration of traditional global power relations has had a dramatic effect on numerous global power brokers. Neoimperialism and unilateralism have become the rallying cries of elites who reject the prospect of emerging global cooperation, power sharing, and even global governance. This eddy is a celebration of self-interest, materialism, and power politics. It is the political counterpart to the economic force of globalizing greed.

Like the Buccaneer, the Hegemon depends directly on the chaotic force of ideological eddies. The offspins of hegemony are many; here are some examples.

The Neoconservative Dream

In curious juxtaposition to neoliberalism, neoconservatism emerged during the Reagan years as the rallying point of what Irving Kristol (one of the movement's founders) famously termed "liberals mugged by reality." Bringing American values and political structures to bear around the world, neoconservatism employs noble-sounding rhetoric in service to an openly aggressive and militaristic global agenda.

Illiberal Democracies

Fareed Zakaria was among the first to call attention to this eddy, illiberal democracies, combining relatively democratic elections with systematic denial of civil liberties. "Democratically elected regimes, often ones that have been reelected or reaffirmed through referenda, are routinely ignoring constitutional limits on their power and depriving their citizens of basic rights and freedoms."[8]

While newer nation-states often make the turn to pseudodemocracy, older, established democracies may turn to illiberalism. Even the United States, during the period of the "war on terror," began to feel the pull of this potentially crippling vortex.

Neoimperialism

The incoming wave in our time suggests that war isn't inevitable, that a new geopolitical multilateralism is possible, and that single-power hegemony is a significant threat. Combined with the palpable decline of the power of the nation-state, this new-wave thinking has given rise to a unique pattern of resistance.

A new imperialism has arisen on the world stage. So aggressive is this new political agenda that it openly embraces the long-despised label of "imperialism." Whether couched in the language of a new American century, the return of Russia to the world stage, or an Islamist world order, neoimperialism is a powerful countercurrent.

Tyranny

When great power and/or great wealth are threatened, tyranny is the expedient response. Moreover, tyranny thrives in a time of uncertainty, when ordinary people come to believe that resistance is futile. Over the last several years, increasing global attention to socioeconomic justice and human rights has prompted gradual relaxation of dictatorships around the world. Several countries, however, have taken the opposite path. Resurgent nationalism (often fueled by ideological fundamentalism and/or fascism) rationalizes tyranny as necessary for state security.

Chauvinism veiled as patriotism enabled Nazi Germany and the Soviet Union to forge eerily similar nationalist totalitarianisms. Tyranny may be the last refuge of concentrated political power in an age of global power sharing, but its eddying potency can't be ignored.

PERCEPTION VERSUS REALITY

What can we conclude? Perhaps the real power of eddies lies in widespread overestimation of their reach. Not only naysayers to cultural evolution fall under the counterevolutionary spell. Many who strongly incline toward new-wave thinking nevertheless may worry overmuch about the threat represented by reactionary value spins like fundamentalism or neoimperialism.

While the possibility exists that a particularly intense eddy—like global terrorism—might spin out of control with terrible consequences, a much better outcome seems highly probable. In general, eddies may well seem more threatening than they actually are. Cultural complexes anchored in discredited ideologies and acquiescence to the wealth and power of shrinking elites seem unlikely to survive the century. And the signs of a genuine transformation are becoming more difficult to ignore.

Next, let's give some thought to the experience of life in a cultural renaissance. In a later chapter, we'll explore the question of how and why eddies dissipate.

To make a coherent life, to confront the terrors of the outer and the inner world, to establish the ritual and art, the pieties and duties which make possible the life of the group and the individual—these are culture, and to contemplate these various enterprises which constitute a culture is inevitably moving.
—Lionel Trilling, *Freud and the Crisis of Our Culture*

And each level of existence, or meme, is more like an emerging wave, a fluid living system, than a rigid hierarchical step. Once a new level appears in a culture, all of the previously acquired developmental stages remain in the composite value system. In Ken Wilber's language, each new social stage "transcends but includes" all of those that have come before. For this reason, the more complex thinking systems have greater degrees of freedom.
—Don Edward Beck, "The Never-Ending Upward Quest"

8

Life in the Renaissance

Despite what you've read, when you watch the news today you may be struck by the chaos and confusion in the world and think accelerated cultural evolution is a distant dream. As we saw in chapter 7, however, many of the most disturbing cultural phenomena of our time belong neither to the older wave nor the newer. They are eddies of resistance to change. Some eddies draw their energy from resentment of the decline of the older values, others from fear of the new. If the cultural evolutionary premise is correct, however, it will become more and more difficult to sustain such whirlpools of opposition.

Still, understanding the forces of resistance may not be enough to persuade you that we're really living through a sea change. Where are the signs that our *culture* itself is undergoing an evolutionary transformation?

These signs aren't always as visible now as they will be in the next decade or so. Remember, ours is not a time of ascendancy of the new wave but a period of crossing. The influence of the rising culture complex is in many ways nearly equal to that of the declining one, but the structures of power are still dominated by the older set of assumptions and behaviors. Nevertheless, the new wave is clearly ascending to take the place of the slowly ebbing tide.

As the two meet and pass, how does culture itself change? In chapter 6, we focused on twenty-first-century value changes, but what are the more concrete signs of change in a culture or a community?

How, in other words, does culture itself change in response to changing values? What will it feel like to live through the shift?

VALUES AND CULTURE

Culture is the organic matrix within which we make our choices and are in turn shaped by them. The culture of a particular society comprises the beliefs, knowledge, practices, and institutions that structure its life and are transmitted to its next generation.

As important as values are, they are only part of the cultural whole. Values change drives cultural change, but think about the relationship between these two dynamics. The benchmarks of a progressive values shift are increasing *creative complexity*, greater awareness of *interdependence*, and the further *integration* of ways of knowing. As these values evolve, what happens to the way people in a culture think and behave?

A good friend once asked me, "How many people do you think lived through the Renaissance?" I've never forgotten his question. He wasn't asking about population figures, but about the atmosphere of the time. How many people knew then that they were witnessing the rediscovery of the human being in relation to the world? How many knew that theirs was an age of revolution? How many woke each morning eager to find out what the next promising development might be or where the next challenge would arise? How many went about their daily tasks simply unaware of the new world taking shape around them? Who responded to new ideas and opportunities? Who exulted?

The situation that confronts us today is similar in many ways. We live in an era in which evolving values are reshaping culture, yet we are often so preoccupied with simply "coping" that we overlook dramatic, positive changes. Instead, we fixate on the seemingly intractable problems that confront us and are drawn into the naysayers' camp.

To grasp what is changing for the better all around us, we need to focus on the relationship between changing values and evolving cultures. With this understanding, we'll be better able to develop strategies for life in a renaissance that's not always apparent.

RENAISSANCE CULTURE

The European Renaissance was named for the "rebirth" of some of the core ideals of classical Greece and Rome. While the term itself may not have been coined until much later, many Italian scholars of the fourteenth and fifteenth centuries seem to have been very aware that they were living at a time of wonderful cultural advance.

The last great sea change was set in motion by the rediscovery of some of the key values of classical antiquity, including its twin fascinations with the human being and with natural philosophy—the precursor of modern science. Is there a parallel "remembrance of things past" in our own Renaissance? Indeed there is. As we've seen, the goods—the initial new wave values of the horizonal sea change—emerge from the preserved bests of earlier cultural transitions. We can discern elements of each prior transitional age in our own crossing. From the Neolithic, for example, we inherit the fascination with technological specialization and the human relationship to the land. We share the Axial concern with ethical obligations toward others in our group. From the modern, of course, we derive much more, including our concern with truth, science, religious and cultural order, and the ideal of fairness.

Many of the new wave values of the current sea change involve some recollection of earlier values. We don't simply return to them, but we come to understand them at deeper levels and employ them in more enlightened ways. In a similar way, scholars of the European Renaissance eagerly sought out the writings of almost forgotten Greek and Roman thinkers. They did not, however, simply absorb those ancient philosophies. They drew them into their own cultural milieu, adapting and refining as they proceeded. Thus, the process of cultural evolution spirals, returning again and again to familiar thematic values and standards, but almost always at a higher level of complexity, insight, and application.

Modeling Cultural Progress

In earlier chapters, we used the two waves, four forces, and three benchmarks to frame the evolution of values in a sea change. Now, we want to focus on the cultural implications of shifting values. What happens to a culture as its respect for ethics or spirituality deepens? What does the renaissance of a long dormant interest in science mean for a culture in transition? What will greater attention to peace, justice, and sustainability mean for our own culture?

In two respects, our investigation has addressed cultural development more directly: 1) the acknowledgement of the roles of yeasayers and naysayers in the current transition, and 2) the analysis of the nature of eddies of resistance. Those are good first steps toward the elucidation of a broader picture of the progress of culture through the advance of values.

Identifying the most characteristic value shifts is essential, but in order to get a more complete sense of our passage, we need a model of the stages of cultural evolution. Throughout human history, thinkers have wrestled with just this problem. Countless theoretical models of cultural evolutionary advance have been propounded just in the last 150 years. One, however, lends itself particularly well to the sea-change hypothesis. It's called "Spiral Dynamics."[1]

THE ASCENDING SPIRAL

Let's take a journey through time. Imagine that we can make a quick survey of several communities over a wide span of human prehistory and

history. The task at each stop is to learn something of the most important cultural values in place and to glimpse the life conditions that gave
rise to those particular values.

- 100,000 years ago: early *Homo sapiens* at the most basic level of human
  social organization, concerned only with survival

- 20,000 years ago: a band of hunters and gatherers with a kinship-
  based social system whose principle value is group belonging

- 8,000 years ago: a group of angry young warriors just break-
  ing free of the constraints of established tribal order, displaying an
  aggressive desire for power and group honor and a disdain for earlier
  egalitarian ways

- 2,000 years ago: an urban community grounded in its certain knowledge of important religious and political truths and cherishing values
  of law, order, faithfulness, etc.

- 120 years ago: a culture at the height of the period of modern triumphalism: prizing science, materialism, competence, pragmatism, and,
  above all, success

- 40 years ago: in the United States, a culture divided by a bitter struggle over essential values, as a new activism confronts war, denial of
  basic human rights, and abuse of the Earth

In each historical period, a significant cultural shift has taken place.
The three benchmarks indicate that the changes have been progressive.
The newer cultural group is more complex than earlier ones. It functions in a more consciously interdependent fashion and displays a greater
integration of knowledge.

At each stage, the process tends to revisit thematic values important
at earlier levels. Each return is likely to embody a higher degree of complexity and a better fit with reality. The circular climb describes a spiral.

Each ascent along that evolutionary spiral brings a culture or community to the next vital stage of maturation.

The Stairway

The Spiral Dynamics system provides insight into the various levels or stages of human cultural development. It is especially useful when discussed in the context of the sea-change model.

Spiral Dynamics describes eight value systems observable in the early twenty-first century—eight stages of development through which evolving cultures must pass. Each stage embodies a broader perspective and a better "fit" with the external world. Each manifests fresh ways of thinking and new priorities. As Ken Wilber puts it, each new social stage "transcends but includes" all of those that have come before. The spiral is the stairway of cultural evolution.

Spiral Dynamics boasts a huge following among cultural evolution's yeasayers, with countless online forums devoted to exploring its nuances and dissecting controversial interpretations. For our purposes, however, a very simplified summary of the model will do. Remember that what we need most is a way to think about the stages of cultural evolution and how cultures at different stages are likely to interact.

The Basics

We begin with several fundamental principles. Cultures differ from one another, sometimes quite dramatically, and a single culture passes through distinct evolutionary stages. Colonial America is not Civil War America; neither one is early twenty-first-century America. "America" evolves.

Cultures are built up in layers; that is, earlier developmental stages are never really lost. They are "transcended but included." It's easy to see this pattern at work in the life of the individual. By the time we reach adulthood, we have gone beyond, but not entirely left behind, the values and behaviors of our youth.

Every culture, of course, is internally divided into more and less evolved groups (each functioning as a subculture in its own right). Antagonism between evolutionary levels within a given society is a serious, but predictable, challenge. The real problem arises when certain groups become arrested, or closed, at a level beyond which the majority of a given population has already advanced.

Each cultural stage is referred to as a "value meme" (often simply "meme"). A term coined to parallel the biological *gene*, a *meme* in the Spiral Dynamics system is a worldview, a set of organizing principles, a mindset affecting not only what people believe but also the way they think and set priorities.

In Spiral Dynamics terms, a value meme is actually a coherent network of countless cultural patterns (memes) that can endure and be propagated. In other words, "value meme" is shorthand for an entire level of cultural development that incorporates a huge array of cultural elements—everything from parenting styles, to morals and religious or political convictions, to stylistic preferences, and so on. Cultures progress in regular order through several stages (value memes). The movement to the next stage is driven by a change in life conditions.

Once a new value meme rises, all of the most visible aspects of a culture—spirituality, art, politics, religion, sports, science, psychology, sociology, economics, etc.—will be significantly influenced by new understandings of the world.

Individuals, communities, and cultures evolve continuously, as their centers of gravity move to more advanced levels. A culture's ascent to the next value meme does not require a sea change. Every sea change, however, will bring countless cultures, communities, subcultures, and individuals to the next value meme.

The Spiral Dynamics model of cultural evolution includes two tiers of progress. The first tier includes six color-coded and well-defined levels of developing complexity. These six describe the great majority of evolving cultural communities in the world. The major difference between the two tiers lies in the fact that the six stages of the first tier tend to regard one another with varying degrees of hostility. The second-tier levels embody the understanding that every value meme has its place in the larger organism that is global human culture. Individuals and groups at these higher levels are committed to furthering the process of evolution for every group, regardless of the stage it currently occupies.

The Stages

Spiral Dynamics breaks down the two tiers of progress into the following eight stages of cultural evolution.

First Tier

Beige: Survival
Beige is the most basic cultural evolutionary stage, with survival as the clan's focus. Key values include food, shelter, security, and procreation. (Corresponds to the 100,000-years-ago early *Homo sapiens* in the introduction to this section.)

Purple: Kin Belonging
The purple meme is the cultural expression of the tribe. Magic, myth, ritual, and group belonging are at its heart. (Cf. 20,000 years ago: the hunter-gatherer band.)

Red: Pride and Power
The red value level is the powerful assertion of self/group dominance in the jungle that is the world. Red's most characteristic features are egocentrism, courage, impulsive behavior, and redemptive violence (fighting the good fight). Mythic/legendary heroes and cruel villains

exemplify the best and worst faces of the red stage. (Cf. 8,000 years ago: the group of angry young men.)

Blue: Truth and Order

The blue meme resonates with authority and order. It gives rise to structures of meaning, truth claims, and true believers. Key values of healthy blue include religious faith, law, patriotism, morality, and loyalty. Unhealthy blue manifestations include fundamentalism, chauvinism, nationalism, ethnic hatred, etc. (Cf. 2,000 years ago: the urban community grounded in "truth.")

Orange: Material Success

The orange stage emerges from the marriage of science, technology, and materialism. It celebrates success, status, the rule of reason, and a dominant marketplace paradigm (usually, capitalism). Orange celebrates the values of competence, hard work, pragmatism, and economic growth. At its best, orange is committed and confident; at its worst, arrogant and venal. (Cf. 120 years ago: the modern culture of success.)

Green: Communitarian Activism

The green meme marks the culmination of the first tier. Egalitarian in character, it brings peace, human rights, and ecological sustainability to the fore as essential cultural values. Healthy green is visionary; unhealthy green is judgmental and even narcissistic. (Cf. 40 years ago: U.S. culture divided—green versus orange/blue.)

Second Tier

Yellow: Integral Flow

In the yellow stage, people are more aware of the intrinsic value of every one of the levels. Each is seen as appropriate to a particular set of living conditions. Yellow understands that we need not be concerned if some cultures or communities operate at levels of lower complexity. For yellow, life is a kaleidoscope of interrelated systems. Knowledge, flexibility, spontaneity, and competence are valued above power, wealth, or status. Yellow is fascinated by human diversity, but fully committed to the human evolutionary project. Yellow has a deeply spiritual character. Only a tiny fraction of the human population regularly functions at the yellow level.

Turquoise: Holistic Vision
Turquoise culture involves an almost mystical awareness of the complete integration of the entire spiral and of all knowledge. At this stage, thinking is fully integral. Like yellow, turquoise is a stage of spiritual breakthrough. Very few individuals access this level.

The Sea Change and the Spiral

This system provides helpful visual and verbal elements to grasp cultural evolution, but we should not dwell too much on its terminology. Value memes are the same as cultural levels. Whether a given stage of cultural development is denoted by the color blue or by terms like *authoritarian* or *order-based* does not matter in the long run. Spiral Dynamics is also a popular model in the academic world, and if you read more on cultural evolution, it's a concept with which you should be familiar.

When you consider our twenty-first-century sea change from a Spiral Dynamics perspective, you see the simultaneous advance of adaptive values, lifting people from their current place in the spiral to the next level and beyond. Most of us on the planet are currently on the evolutionary path from red, toward blue, toward orange, toward green, toward yellow.

While the United States is home to several competing cultural complexes, or value memes, our cultural center is in the blue-orange-green (truth-success-community) continuum. The current value shift, however, will lift all levels, with the exception of the pockets of deepest resentment and resistance.

Values and Levels

From the perspective of the spiral, the most enduring values in human culture are likely to be interpreted differently at each level of cultural evolutionary advance. Consider the Golden Rule. Treating others as one would wish to be treated sounds like a straightforward proposition, and it is, provided we are agreed on the definition of "other." In many cultures, the Golden Rule would apply only to members of one's own family, village, or ethnic group. Applying the principle to the entire human community happens at a fairly advanced stage of cultural development. Applying it to other species takes us to still another level.

We might also ask what "fairness" means at different points along the human cultural continuum. At the red level of aggressive individualism, it may mean a fair fight. At the blue stage of concern with truth and order, it may mean a fair hearing of competing arguments. For materialistically interested orange, it may mean a fair contract or fair division of profits. For communitarian green, it may take the form of fairness and justice for all. For evolutionary yellow, what's most important is the ability to grasp the complex interplay of all these interpretations. That understanding can help resolve conflicts and promote human growth.

YEAS AND NAYS: THE INFRASTRUCTURES

I recall a long conversation I had with a close friend when this book was just a germ of an idea. She told me she desperately wanted to believe there might be something to the notion of sea change but just couldn't make the leap. She returned again and again to the same wistful refrain: "How can you possibly believe that things are changing for the better?" Ironically, my friend is a young Latin American who has been at the forefront of the movement for global peace, justice, and ecological good sense. She and her colleagues are some of the finest exemplars of twenty-first-century sea change. Yet, although she loved the concept, her experience made her hesitate. She focused on two particularly disturbing patterns: fundamentalist extremism and the rampant globalization of greed in the desperate race to Americanize the planet. These reactionary patterns impede her work for a better world.

Understandably, she has assumed that these negative trends were the *real* manifestations of the coming world order. As we sat together and reviewed the two decades of her own experience as an agent of dramatic change, she began to acknowledge that she, rather than those destructive whirlpools of resistance, represented the wave of the future. Today, she's an enthusiastic sea changer, fully persuaded that cultural evolution is already beginning to dissipate some of the whirlpools of resistance. Her turn from nay to yea captures the spirit of a time of genuine cultural advance—a renaissance.

In chapter 1, we discussed the yeasayers and the naysayers and their very different responses to the idea that ours is a time of momentous cultural transformation. If significant groups support or oppose the idea that ours is a very special time, then we should be able to identify important *infrastructures* of change and resistance in modern culture.

We'll take up that question shortly. First, it will be useful to quickly review the *Yea-Nay* matrix.

As we saw in chapter 1, scholars on each side of the cultural evolution debate and advance important arguments. However, a survey of the literature makes it very clear that the preponderance of scholarly weight is with the yeas. In fact, the skeptics tend largely to find fault with particular approaches, rather than with the evolutionary concept itself.

My young Latin friend's change of heart demonstrates the eagerness of many disillusioned activists (Left Fielders) to believe again and to join in the evolutionary struggle, as the shift becomes more apparent. Moreover, what many are calling the return of the grand narrative signals a weakening of academic resistance to hopeful theories like sea change.

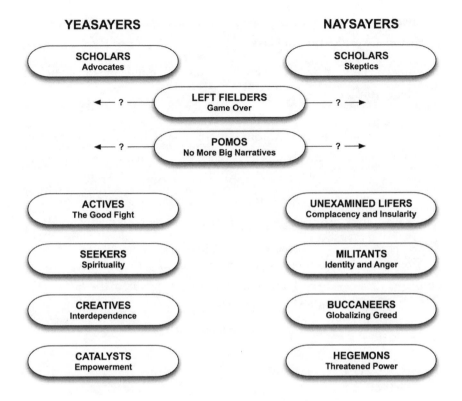

Figure 8.1. Living in a Time of Cultural Evolution?

But in any case, the real yea-nay tension involves neither the scholars nor the skeptics. It is not a conceptual disagreement, but a clash of values. The yeasayer is not only persuaded by the argument, but also committed to the evolutionary advance it represents. The naysayer is unlikely to contest the theory intellectually, but is deeply fearful of what it may mean.

Note that each Yea is opposed by a Nay.

- fighting for change (Actives) versus fighting against it (Militants)

- pursuing understanding (Seekers) versus passive isolation (Unexamined Lifers)

- creating networks of abundance (Creatives) versus accumulating material wealth (Buccaneers)

- empowering others (Catalysts) versus pursuing personal power (Hegemons)

These intergroup oppositions mirror a deeper divide in the culture itself. Each of the two sides (yeasayers and naysayers) represents a network of cultural subgroups. An array of infrastructures supports each network and propagates its responses to evolutionary change. We'll take a brief look at several representative infrastructures of change and resistance.

I've chosen only three exemplars from each category. There are, of course, countless others. These six, however, are paradigmatic. As was the case with the Yeas and Nays, each infrastructure of change (wellspring) meets a parallel infrastructure of resistance (sinkhole).

- Web 2.0 versus enclaves of isolation

- the new story versus narratives of denial

- bottom-up globalization versus top-down globalization

Wellsprings of Change

First, we'll consider three yeas that energize the horizonal sea change. While the Italian Renaissance embraced new visual modes of expression, our own era has developed creative ways to interact and to build community at every level. In the early twenty-first century, the global reach of telecommunications is staggering, as is the list of its modalities: telephone, radio, television, facsimile transmission, cellular connectivity, and the World Wide Web and its offspring—email, search engines, online data archives, weblogs, social networking media, and so much more.

Each of the following is an aspect of our own Renaissance. Each is a bountiful source of evolutionary complexity, interdependence, and knowledge integration. And each in its own way relies on global communication and collaboration systems that are still emerging.

Web 2.0

The widely heralded second generation of Web development goes beyond the static presentation of information on Web pages. What's already taking shape (in a classic self-organizing, complexity-increasing way) is a highly interactive system. One of the most intriguing features of this next iteration of life on the Internet involves social networking media. Allowing for easy collaboration, pursuit of shared interests, and information sharing, the new media has given rise to hundreds of thousands of virtual communities. That Web 2.0 is already facilitating the complex, interdependent networking that is becoming a signature of the new wave becomes clearer every day.

The New Story

In chapter 9, we'll explore the idea of the "new story"—the mythic tale for our time. For now we can say that it is an account of the power of evolution to shape our world and our cultural lives toward increasing complexity, consciousness, and cooperation. Various forms of the new story are taking shape in most of the world's guiding institutions—including religion, government, business, the arts and communications media, education, science, intergovernmental organizations, and civil society. It usually comes in the form of a call to action, grounded in the belief that we live in an age of tremendous challenge and marvelous opportunity. Whatever the source of the new narrative, it almost certainly identifies significant problems facing the planetary community (anomalies), shares news of best practices or what's making a difference around the world (*ahas*), and warns of dangerous patterns of opposition to evolutionary progress (eddies). The spread of the new story is one of the most important and most overlooked dimensions of the age.

Bottom-Up Globalization

When we think of globalization, we tend to visualize global markets and the movement of vast amounts of money, goods, and services around the world. But the global village has another dimension that may in the long run prove more transformative than the purely economic version. Facilitated by the same new global interconnectedness, globalization from the bottom up is concerned with countering the negative effects of the Northernization of the world. Globalization's cheerleaders, busy celebrating the new "flat" world and its business-friendly atmosphere, usually ignore the many victims of the process. But a remarkable self-organizing network of committed individuals and groups has emerged over the past two decades. It's a movement dedicated to combating poverty, promoting universal primary education, empowering women, promoting appropriate technology, teaching environmental stewardship, advancing nonviolent conflict resolution, and countless other projects. Although we don't hear much about it on a daily basis, bottom-up globalization is without question one of the most vital of the new wellsprings of global cultural evolution.

With so much momentum coming from the energetic wellsprings, then, why isn't the world simply changing overnight? Where is the renaissance when we really need it? The answers lie in a declining modern value system that still has tremendous inertial resistance to evolutionary movement.

Sinkholes of Resistance

Like most of the wellsprings of change, some of the sinkholes of resistance rely heavily on telecommunications. These forms of obstruction (like the eddies they help to create) begin to weaken as their disconnect with reality becomes more apparent. Each of the anti-evolutionary sinkholes moves the affected cultural subgroup toward decreased complexity, diminished awareness of interdependence, and the disintegration of knowledge.

Enclaves of Isolation

The favored abode of many Unexamined Lifers and Militants, the enclave is always a real or virtual territory whose inhabitants are set apart culturally from the surrounding region. Religious and cultural exclusivism creates a sense of separateness that often takes shape in increasing social and physical isolation from the larger world. Religious fundamentalism frequently counsels detachment from the "profane" world. When an enclave is no longer open to new information or understanding—when it ignores anomalies and disdains *ahas*—it is effectively cut off from cultural evolution. That phenomenon is a major source of active opposition to evolutionary progress and of some of the most destructive eddies in the current crossing.

Narratives of Denial

We have become sadly familiar with the litany of denials: of the theory of evolution, of the Holocaust, of anthropogenic climate change, of systemic poverty and injustice, of the usefulness of stem-cell research, of gender equity, of racial equality, of homosexual rights. The list goes on and on. What's at work here is not, however, simple skepticism or thoughtful intellectual opposition. Even a cursory examination of most of these positions reveals deliberate distortion and manipulation. Narratives of denial have become a basic currency of exchange between important concentrations of anti-evolutionary power on the one hand and the enclaves of cultural confusion and identity crisis on the other. Whether one wishes to manipulate the red-state voter, the devout Muslim middle class, or the angry white male, the narrative of denial is a powerful tool. The villain is always the same: a mysterious elite class that despises the hard work and simple values of real people. It's worth noting that, while the denial of biological evolution is just one item on the list, every other, in its own way, denies human cultural evolution. A strategy that rests on the continuing repudiation of the increasingly obvious doesn't have a long-term future. Nevertheless, this infrastructure of resistance has already birthed a huge number of extremely destructive eddies.

Top-Down Globalization

Globalization from the top down is usually identified with the Americanization or Northernization of global exchange. In fact, it often affects not only economic realities, but cultural patterns as well. The process has largely been shaped by free-market capitalism and the so-called neoliberal economic philosophy. Both systems argue that wealth and power are most equitably distributed when economic exchange is unregulated and unhindered by artificial structures. In practice, top-down globalization is exploited by the wealth and power seekers of the late modern value age (the Buccaneers and Hegemons in our list of naysayers). Attempts to reform global trade, to institute wiser environmental and labor practices, or to safeguard the global commons, for example, have met with powerful opposition from these quarters. While it is often argued that globalization from the top down increases intercultural connectedness, activists from the global South (like Vandana Shiva, India; Walden Bello, the Philippines; Martin Khor, Malaysia; and Oronto Douglas, Nigeria) make a strong counterargument. They note that the exchange tends to be one-way, with American and European goods, cuisine, and culture overwhelming local patterns and eliminating many essential elements of regional and ethnic society. The one-way process reduces complexity and substitutes dependence for interdependence.

Postscript

In chapter 9, we'll take a much closer look at one of the most important wellsprings of change: the opening of a "Second Axial Age," a spiritual transformation that may even eclipse the First Axial Age (the second sea change). One may well ask, however, since the phenomenon of a cultural evolutionary leap is so multifaceted, why we should direct our attention to one particular aspect, and a spiritual one at that?

If you'll recall, I suggested that the still emerging higher stages of cultural evolution (the yellow and the turquoise in Spiral Dynamics terms) are spiritual in nature. That is not meant to suggest adherence to any particular religious belief or to any religion at all. Instead, in the context of our exploration "spiritual" means open to the possibility of extraordinary growth in complexity, consciousness, and compassion. It means, above all, conscious evolution.

Sea change, like cultural evolution, *is* a spiritual phenomenon. It touches the deepest roots of our inner life, our most profound connectedness with one another, and our furthest-reaching insights into the universe. It seems fitting, therefore, for the great physicist Albert Einstein to provide the bridge to a deeper discussion of the spiritual dimension of our Renaissance. Though he made it quite clear that he did not believe in a God concerned with the fates of humans, Einstein often spoke of the "mystical" or of the "cosmic religious feeling." He wrote, in *The Merging of Spirit and Science*, "The most beautiful and most profound experience is the sensation of the mystical. It is the sower of all true science. He to whom this emotion is a stranger, who can no longer wonder and stand rapt in awe, is as good as dead. To know that what is impenetrable to us really exists, manifesting itself as the highest wisdom and the most radiant beauty which our dull faculties can comprehend only in their primitive forms—this knowledge, this feeling is at the center of true religiousness."[2]

All the religions and all the peoples of the world are undergoing the most radical, far-reaching, and challenging transformation in history. . . . Forces, which have been at work for centuries, have in our day reached a crescendo that has the power to draw the human race into a global network and the religions of the world into a global spiritual community.

—Ewert Cousins, "Religions of the World"

All over the world, people are struggling with these new conditions and have been forced to reassess their religious traditions, which were designed for a very different type of society. They are finding that the old forms of faith no longer work for them; they cannot provide the enlightenment and consolation that human beings seem to need. As a result . . . they are attempting to build upon the insights of the past in a way that will take human beings forward into the new world they have created for themselves.

—Karen Armstrong, "A New Axial Age"

— 9 —

The Second Axial Age

The second of the great sea changes was the passage into the Axial Age, in the first millennium BCE. The rise of the classical religious traditions advanced apace with the development of individual consciousness. Ethical awareness and the spiritual search shaped this earlier sea change, as the late theologian Ewert Cousins describes:

> The Axial Period ushered in a radically new form of consciousness. Whereas primal consciousness was tribal, Axial consciousness was individual. "Know thyself" became the watchword of Greece; the Upanishads identified the *atman*, the transcendent center of the self. The Buddha charted the way of individual enlightenment; the Jewish prophets awakened individual moral responsibility. This sense of individual identity, as distinct from the tribe and from nature, is the most characteristic mark of Axial consciousness. From this flow other characteristics: consciousness that is self-reflective, analytic, and that can be applied to nature in the form of scientific theories, to society in the form of social critique, to knowledge in the form of philosophy, to religion in the form of mapping an individual spiritual journey.[1]

Our twenty-first-century sea change is ushering in its own "great transformation," which Cousins and others have described as a Second

Axial Period. The Second Axial turning is simply the horizonal sea change viewed from a religious and/or spiritual perspective. An ancient parable from the Hindu mythic tradition illustrates one of the core values of this Second Axial Period: adherents of the great traditions converge as their understanding deepens. It's another example of the best values of past sea changes reappearing in a novel form as the goods of a newer shift.

While the twenty-first-century crossing has countless aspects—social, political, ecological, economic, etc.—I've chosen to focus on its spiritual dimension. Arguably the most important change underway in our time is the change in our most profound values, perceived truths that shape our most essential attitudes and choices. Whether or not a person is religious, he or she has a spiritual dimension. A global change in these deepest structures of meaning will have tremendous implications.

THE SACRED WHEEL

Imagine a great wheel whose immense and beautifully carved spokes converge in a tiny glistening hub. In the Hindu tradition, the wheel is a symbol of human spiritual search and discovery. Each of the uniquely shaped and decorated spokes symbolizes one of the world's religious paths. The rim of the wheel represents the most superficial level of understanding of any tradition. It's the level at which the religions are most dramatically separated from one another by their distinctions. Conversely, the hub is the center from which each spoke emerges and the point at which all come together. It represents the common source and the deepest level of each and every tradition.

As the seeker grows in understanding, he or she moves along one of the spokes, from the gigantic rim to the small hub at the center. At the rim, the spokes are widely separated, but as they converge on the center of the hub, separation all but vanishes.

As I stand on the rim at the outer end, say, of the Christian spoke and gaze across at my Buddhist counterparts, their faith seems strange, if not bizarre. And yet, as I begin to move along my own spoke, the distance that had divided us begins to diminish.

As I venture more deeply into my own tradition, learning something of its symbolic language and hidden dimensions, I begin to see the Buddhist symbols as kindred to my own. Suddenly, it's clear that our paths are convergent, sharing a common center. Just as the wagon wheel needs both its circles—the rim and the hub—so the symbolic wheel of human spirituality requires the diversity, the color, the pageantry, and variety of the outer circle as well as the harmony of the inner. But it is convergence, "inclining to a center," that makes a wheel a wheel.

The image of the sacred wheel is powerful because it gives us a way to think about a spiritual sea change. More specifically, it describes the essential processes of this Second Axial Age: encountering *diversity*, beginning a cross-cultural *dialogue*, and discovering the possibilities inherent in interreligious *engagement*.

The Encounter with Diversity

As I've noted, religions in the twentieth and twenty-first centuries discovered each other as never before. The United States, as Diana Eck has demonstrated, is the most religiously diverse country on the planet.[2] Chicago is one of the most religiously diverse cities. And neighborhoods around the world have unquestionably attained a greater religious heterogeneity. The other is now much likelier to be an acquaintance or a friend. This development reveals the connection between biological and cultural evolution.

Biology equipped human beings with the survival mechanism known as the fright-flight-fight response. In the presence of perceived danger, a complex of biological systems—from heart rate and blood pressure to adrenaline production—kicks in. We prepare to confront a perceived threat. This biological response, however, is a bit out of date today. Most of our biologically evolved patterns belong to the environment of evolutionary adaptedness—the period, from 1.5 to 2.5 million years ago in which the genus *Homo* emerged and began to evolve. In that long-ago era, the stranger coming over the hill likely meant danger.

But our definition of "stranger" has changed dramatically since those earliest days. Cultural evolution moves at a far faster pace than its biological analog. The most adaptable communities might well have been those that narrowed the cultural category of "stranger" while broadening those of "neighbor" or "friend." This evolutionary advance did not occur in the exchange of genes but in the circulation of memes. As we saw in chapter 8, memes are the cultural units of transmission that mirror the function of genes in biological evolution and development. Some of the most influential memes take form in myths, stories, legends, and religious parables. In this context the stranger becomes the neighbor and the neighbor the friend. The biological fright-flight-fight complex remains intact. It is simply less likely to be activated in the presence of the unknown other.

Our responses to stimuli are slow to change, but our recognition and classification of a given stimulus is likely to reside in the domain of culture. Changing human behavior by altering biology (through drug therapy, etc.) may prove to be far less effective than the approach through culture, and especially through dialogue and engagement with the religious and cultural other.

Interreligious Dialogue

The great Jewish thinker Martin Buber, author of *I and Thou*, often recalled his first experience of what he called "feeling the other side." On a farm in the German countryside, he was brushing and currying a dapple-grey horse. As her breathing changed in response to the strokes, Buber suddenly felt as though he had changed places with the animal. Although his own arms continued their rhythmic movement, he now began to feel the currying as if he were the recipient. In a sense, he "became" the horse and shared its experience. In that moment, the vision of interfaith encounter that would shape so much of Buber's life and work began to emerge.[3]

We may often wonder if real dialogue is possible with other faiths and with individuals whose religious identity differs so sharply from our own. Buber's experience, though, combined with the imagery of the sacred wheel, provides a sense of new possibilities in this Second Axial Age, a way to experience the other side and then to engage with the other.

Interreligious Engagement

To engage with the religious other involves seeking out shared values and cooperating to create a better world. Each of this chapter's epigraphs suggests the possibility of interreligious understanding, harmony, and cooperation for the common good. As our cultural sea change continues to unfold, religious communities and multireligious partnerships are finding new ways to pursue these possibilities.

Thousands of religious and interreligious groups, NGOs, and ad hoc collaboratives are working around the world on projects addressing human rights and social justice, the empowerment of women, ecological sustainability, sustainable development, and the creation of cultures of peace. Several of the groups mentioned in chapter 6 are particularly active in projects of this kind (e.g., World Religions for Peace, the International Interreligious Peace Council, the Council for a Parliament of the World's Religions, and the United Religions Initiative).

THE SECOND AXIAL TURNING

To understand this new Axial Age, we need to understand the first. Though separated by more than two thousand years, the two are strikingly parallel. As you'll recall, the previous Axial Age—the second sea change we discussed—produced the great classical religious traditions. It also encouraged the development of human consciousness from the tribal to the individual, nurtured the notion of transcendence, and catalyzed ethical and spiritual growth.

In the First Axial Period, *individual* consciousness emerged, allowing people to distinguish themselves from a purely tribal identity. Our own Second Axial Age nurtures a new *global* consciousness. We are still acutely, individually aware, but we are beginning to recognize our roles as global beings. Ewert Cousins was perhaps the first thinker to bring the idea of a Second Axial Age into sharp focus.

> If we shift our gaze from the first millennium BCE to the eve of the twenty-first century, we can discern another transformation of consciousness. It is so profound and far-reaching that I call it the Second Axial Period. Like the first it is happening simultaneously around the earth, and like the first it will shape the horizon of consciousness for future centuries. Not surprisingly, too, it will have great significance for world religions, which were constituted in the First Axial Period. However, the new form of consciousness is different from that of the First Axial Period. Then it was individual consciousness, now it is global consciousness.[4]

The Second Axial Age represents a return to some of the values that shaped the first, especially in terms of spiritual renewal. This modern phenomenon involves a profound deepening of spiritual practice. Something remarkable is underway in the world's great traditions: religious and spiritual reform, renewal, and revival are emerging on every side. Intriguingly, spiritual renewal turns out to be a strongly cross-cultural and cross-traditional phenomenon. Buddhists and Catholics, Muslims and Jews, Christians and humanists are increasingly engaging as spiritual coexplorers.

Two Revolutions

The great religions today continue to be guided in large measure by the vision of First Axial founders and communities. For the most part, Second Axial values do not depart in any major ways from those foundational insights and teachings. Instead, they call us back to our roots even as they point the way ahead.

Our own Second Axial Age adds several additional vital features to the individual consciousness that emerged in the first age. Most important is the transition from exclusivism (complete denial of the truth of the other) toward inclusivism (acknowledgment of the possibility that the other's truth may be an acceptable subset or variant of one's own, superior, truth) toward pluralism (openness to the possibility that religious truth, as symbolic expression, may be found in many cultures and traditions).

Moreover, religion and spirituality in the current crossing are increasingly engaged with the great issues of the age: nonviolence and the building of cultures of peace, the nurturing of economic and social justice and human rights, and honoring and preserving the Earth and all her life systems. Not surprisingly, many aspects of the challenges facing the Second Axial are legacies of the first. The uncompromising religious monologues and unfeeling patriarchal structures that mar so much of the modern religious landscape are inheritances from that first turning three thousand years ago.

AT THE CUTTING EDGE

The idea of a Second Axial Age provides a way to discern and to savor the profound spiritual dimension of the horizonal crossing. Remember that when we speak of a Second Axial Age, we're actually taking a much closer look at one of the most vital dimensions of our current sea change. In the following sections, we'll explore this spiritual dimension, and in so doing, we'll open an unparalleled panorama of the twenty-first-century sea change. The view may in fact be as intriguing to the nonbeliever or the agnostic as it is to the spiritual seeker.

Are You Fluent in Symbolic?

The difference between life at the outer rim or nearer the hub of the sacred wheel lies in sensitivity to symbolic expression. The two rim dwellers we imagined earlier cannot understand each other's words or ritual practices because they don't grasp the language of symbols. For them, all religious expression is literal: mythless, symbol-free, and utterly lacking in metaphor and allegory.

In a religious world without symbol, one cannot even hint at the ineffable, and Buddha can never be "a finger pointing at the Moon." To appreciate the poverty of religion devoid of its symbolic dimension, imagine an entire culture based on the strictest literalism, devoid of the imagistic wordplay on which not only religion but also poetry and humor depend. Mr. Data, *Star Trek*'s cyberhumanoid, could neither tell nor get a joke. Surely he would struggle with the late philosopher René Dubos' observation that "both the myths of religion and the laws of science, it is now becoming apparent, are not so much descriptions of facts as symbolic expressions of cosmic truths."[5]

But there is hope for the rim folk of every religious tradition. Each spoke of the sacred wheel—each path—is designed to draw us deeper into the rich, consciousness-expanding world of symbolic words, gestures, rituals, and experiences. To a new generation of Second Axial spiritual explorers, awareness of the symbolic expression of those teachings is becoming second nature. As the Dalai Lama explains, religions use conventional or relative expressions to speak of absolute truth, which can be experienced but not spoken. In the Second Axial Period, we'll no longer assume that only a single religion can be valid; we'll come to embrace the notion that many religions *point* faithfully at the truth of human existence.

Myth and the New Story

The mythologist Joseph Campbell fervently believed that the world needed and was in the process of creating new myths that would guide humankind through the twenty-first century. He understood that myths are *not* old, false tales, but often-vibrant conduits for passing on cultural and spiritual insights.

Campbell also grasped that while the old myths still possessed immense power to instruct, they were the products of a distant time. He argued that we urgently need a new story that will put the ancient mythic themes—individual maturation, the hero's journey, the relation to society, and facing the end—into the context of what we know today about the Earth and all life. In his celebrated dialogue with Bill Moyers, recorded near the end of Campbell's life, he said, "The only myth that's going to be worth thinking about in the immediate future is one talking about the planet."

The new myth that Campbell anticipated is already being told in convergent forms around the world. In their *The Universe Story*, physicist Brian Swimme and the late Thomas Berry, pioneer of the eco-spiritual movement, offered one of the first iterations of an emerging mythology for the new Axial Age. The "new story" they tell is a captivating account of our "time-developmental" universe, and its increasingly complex and marvelous cosmic, physical, biological, and cultural evolution.

Noting that the old stories still have immense value, Swimme points out that they can no longer give us an accurate account of the universe and the human condition as we know them today. "We have discovered more about life in the last 100 years than in the whole of prior human history. . . . But we haven't yet learned to live within that knowledge. . . . We need a new story. . . . We're in that exciting stage of entering a new way of being human, which requires a new story, a new account of what it *means* to be human."[6]

The sea-change hypothesis needs to be understood as another version of that new story. It functions as a mythic tale of the evolution of the universe, inspiring us as well as providing a map to guide us on the journey.

Deep Dialogue

For Leonard Swidler, the Second Axial Age is the age of dialogue, replacing the age of monologue ushered in by the First Axial Revolution. Founder and director of the Dialogue Institute at Temple University, he developed the "seven stages of deep dialogue," a model that has gained significant global acceptance.

In a shorter form of the seven stages, Swidler draws on the thought of Teilhard de Chardin to describe the openhearted encounter between individuals from different religious traditions as "dialogic dialogue," which he contrasts with "dialectic dialogue," the polemic challenge to the other. In real dialogue, we can observe three key events:

1. The partners meet each other in an atmosphere of mutual understanding, ready to alter misconceptions about each other and eager to appreciate the values of the other.

2. The partners are mutually enriched, by passing over into the consciousness of the other so that each can experience the other's values from within the other's perspective.

3. If such a creative union is achieved, then the religions will have moved into the more complex yet unifying form of consciousness that will be characteristic of the twenty-first century.[7]

In Swidler's view, the movement toward real dialogue is the distinguishing feature of the Second Axial Age. Leaving behind the countless competing religious monologues, First Axial legacies, we enter the age of dialogue.

The shift from dialectic to dialogic in interreligious relations may prove to be one of the most significant drivers of the larger cultural sea change. When Mohammad Khatami, former president of Iran, called for a "global dialogue of civilizations," he offered a compelling alternative to historian Samuel Huntington's widely discussed impending "clash of civilizations." Huntington saw religion as the principle defining aspect of a culture or civilization. Therefore, Khatami's challenge was particularly meaningful. If religions can master the challenge of authentic dialogue, then not only they, but global culture itself will take the path of dialogue.

The New Liberation

Religion and spirituality today are often intertwined with efforts for peace, justice, and ecological sustainability, and this convergence is another signal that the Second Axial Age is dawning. Consider liberation theology, born in the late 1960s in Latin America in the wake of the Second Vatican Council. Dedicated to the cause of social and economic justice, and what it termed "the preferential option for the poor," the movement had many dedicated intellectual architects (Gustavo Gutierrez, Jon Sobrino, Leonardo Boff, and many other religious leaders in Latin America). It sought to reconcile Christianity with Marxist theory, but its most characteristic expression was in the "base communities," local Christian groups that practiced a bottom-up approach to scripture, the resolution of moral issues, and spiritual life.

Declared dead by some skeptical conservatives (of the religious and political varieties), the liberation movement still is very much alive globally, if somewhat more diffuse than in the past. Deeply interreligious, liberation is observable in countless local and regional initiatives.

Interreligious groups like the United Religions Initiative, World Religions for Peace, and Globalization for the Common Good, aided by the global increase in intercultural awareness, work to advance the cause of justice and human rights. Of particular importance is that religious proselytizing has, at least in the developing interreligious context, given way to service to the poor and oppressed people of the world.

We've already explored the central importance of justice and human rights as a core value of the horizonal sea change. But we need to realize the power of religion (so often misused as a tool of oppression) as a potentially vital wellspring of inspiration and energy in the struggle for justice. Even those who see religion as a form of human blindness or cognitive dysfunction are likely to admit that its power for good should not be lightly dismissed.

In 1965, Americans witnessed an early manifestation of the interreligious movement. On March 21, Rabbi Abraham Joshua Heschel and the Reverend Martin Luther King, Jr., led thousands of marchers across the Pettus Bridge from Selma to Montgomery, Alabama. It's hard to imagine the civil rights movement as a purely secular affair.

Reclaiming the Feminine

The sea change associated with the First Axial Age, like all major cultural evolutionary shifts, eventually disclosed its darker aspects. One, as Swidler has shown, was a world dominated by competing religious and cultural monologues. Another was the universal ascent of the patriarchal order, replacing what may well have been fairly widespread egalitarian gender norms. The great traditions all seem to have succumbed to the male-dominance paradigm that is still preeminent, though dramatically eroding, in religions today.

The Feminenza Network ("an international network of women formed in April 2000, working in 16 countries with a view to pioneering a new template for women") describes the healing process: "The establishment of basic human rights for women (at least in the West) that has occurred in the last 100 years can be perceived as restoring a more natural state of affairs between men and women that started to go wrong during the start of what some historians call 'The Axial Age.'"[8]

Women's reempowering represents a transformative aspect of the current cultural evolutionary flux. Swidler notes that the end of the age of monologue emerged first in an interreligious context, but eventually affected the entire spectrum of the global culture shift. In the same way, a transformation of women's role in religious institutions *and* of the feminine in spirituality is a major marker not only of the Second Axial shift but also of the entire twenty-first-century sea change.

Is the Planet Really Sacred?

Thomas Berry thought so. Before his death in 2009, Berry had become one of the most important religious voices addressing the human relationship to the Earth and the planetary community. In *Evening Thoughts: Reflecting on Earth as Sacred Community*, he wrote: "The ancient human-Earth relationship must be recovered in a new context, in its mystical as well as in its physical functioning. There is need for awareness that the mountains and rivers and all living things, the sky and its sun and moon and clouds all constitute a healing, sustaining sacred presence for humans which they need as much for their psychic integrity as for their physical nourishment."[9]

While some environmentalists and ecologists believe that religion has always been bad for the Earth, that is not the case. Early religious expressions viewed the physical world as animated or ensouled, an honored dwelling place for divinities and spirits as well as for humans and other life forms. Indigenous reverence for the Earth and other species survives today in many cultures, though often in a deteriorated form.

The passage to modernity, however, gave rise, particularly in the European world, to a hostile cultural and religious attitude toward the natural order. New religious teachings spoke of the human and the natural realms as locked in endless struggle, of the human "conquest" of the world, and of physical existence as the domain of Satan rather than of God. While notions of this sort began to lose their power as early as the nineteenth century, religions have too often been silent on humankind's moral obligations with respect to nature.

Inspired by the work of Thomas Berry and others, an extraordinary project took shape in the mid-1990s. The Forum on Religion and Ecology, organized by Mary Evelyn Tucker and John Grim, brought together a series of ten conferences, each representing one of the world's great religious traditions. Ten volumes of conference proceedings followed. This massive undertaking produced the first authoritative compendium of the beliefs of the world's religions on the human relationship to nature. It has inspired countless vision-to-action projects on the part of religious and interreligious groups around the world.

Many religious activists have contributed to the ecological awakening that will be remembered as a Second Axial signature. The importance of the work of the Forum, however, lies in its demonstration that the world's religions have reflected long and deeply on the human-nature dynamic.

We Are Not Alone

The changing relationships among the world's religious traditions clearly signal the arrival of a Second Axial Age. Having been involved in interreligious dialogue and engagement for the past twenty years, I've witnessed an almost unparalleled cultural evolution in this arena.

In his *Christians and Religious Pluralism*, the noted British theologian Alan Race proposed an extremely useful typology for describing the range of religious responses to the fact that more than one religion exists. He suggests three important theological positions: exclusivism, inclusivism, and pluralism.[10] For over twenty-five years, this threefold scheme has been at the center of one of the most fascinating debates in the fields of religion and theology:

- Exclusivism, very simply put, is the view that the truth of my religious belief and practice demands that yours be false. Exclusivism has been the dominant pattern of belief about the religious other throughout all but the most recent fraction of human history. But it's getting harder and harder to maintain. The problem is that the absolute denial of another's religious or spiritual truth usually demands that I know almost nothing about it. That's not as easy as it was for my grandmother.

- Inclusivism holds that, while my position is superior, yours may be adequate (as a somewhat deficient variant of my own) to provide for your salvation, enlightenment, etc. In a major Pew Forum survey released in 2009, 70 percent of religiously affiliated Americans stated that many religions can lead to eternal life. This survey supports the argument that exclusivism is declining in our globalizing world. Inclusivism, on the other hand, has drawn significant strength from the global interreligious movement.

- The third position differs dramatically from the others, since they are *beliefs* about the truth while pluralism is a philosophical hypothesis. In essence, it proposes that more than one religion can be perfectly valid. Pluralism is not relativism, since it is willing to argue that certain religious arguments are simply not coherent. The true pluralist is distinguished not by the certainty that others are (at least partly) wrong, but by the willingness to accept that they (and many others) may be right. The Second Axial Revolution may eventually embrace the *pluralist* hypothesis.

Unquestionably, however, a new spirit of interreligious inclusivism and pluralism is abroad in a world in which, not so long ago, one's religious identity was almost always exclusionary in nature. I was raised as a Roman Catholic in a world in which everyone was either Catholic or non-Catholic. It was a major revelation to discover that there were *no* "non-Catholics"—that no one had non-Catholic as a self-identity.

Consider a small thought experiment. Imagine that we have gathered together five religious progressives and five fundamentalists, one of each from five different traditions. A simple multiple-choice test administered to the participants will almost certainly reveal that the progressives have more in common with one another than any one has with the fundamentalist from his or her tradition. Conversely, fundamentalists from different faiths are likelier to have more in common with one another than with their progressive coreligionists. An intriguing Second Axial development seems to be a tendency toward what some are already calling post-denominationalism. This is not intended to deny the uniqueness of a given path, but rather to emphasize that denominational unity on which exclusivism has traditionally depended might become more elusive.

In fact, each of the Second Axial spheres discussed plays a role in the decline of exclusivism and its enclaves. We know more about one another and about other cultures than has ever been possible in human history. Exclusivism, by definition, will seem less and less plausible.

CODA: MILESTONES

A few years ago I asked my distinguished artist friend Lonnie Hanzon to sketch some simple diagrams of the gradual progression of interreligious engagement. I gave him the names of ten successive stages (all gradations of the threefold typology exclusivism-inclusivism-pluralism). His quick sketches have forever altered my way of thinking about the relations between and among the religions. I hope that these drawings will become iconic. They capture the spirit of the long passage from the First Axial Age to the Second with wit and clarity. And they provide a useful guide for reflection on one's own changing attitudes toward the religious or cultural other.

Religions (or cultures) can interrelate in countless ways. This model offers glimpses of ten. The first column represents the modes of their separation. The second traces the ascending degrees of interreligious (and intercultural) engagement.

Figure 9.1. Modes of Interreligious Alienation and Engagement (original art by Lonnie Hanzon)

Progressive thought rests, first, on the value of empathy—putting oneself in other people's shoes, seeing the world through their eyes, and therefore caring about them. The second principle is acting on that care, taking responsibility both for oneself and others, social as well as individual responsibility. The third is acting to make oneself, the country, and the world better.

—George Lakoff, "The Obama Code"

Can we evolve fast enough?. . . I do sense that the possibility for the evolution of human consciousness is absolutely at hand. . . . Much has already taken place. Alternative ways of being that have grown up on the periphery of our society and of societies around the world are now coming into the center and being valued: ecological economics, green politics, alternative technologies, sustainable farming, etc. . . . This suggests that evolution is very much in process and in progress. . . . I think we can do it.

—Mary Evelyn Tucker, "Can We Evolve Fast Enough?"

— 10 —

Thriving in the Crosscurrent

The most critical existential moment of life in the time of crossing comes when one realizes that it has actually arrived. It's no longer "coming" or "fast approaching," It's here. Old cultural patterns decline in influence, though often retaining at least inertial energy. Still-viable traditional values are transformed, often in surprising ways. New values, new ways of thinking, and new priorities increase in influence. Self-organizing structures of understanding and behavior emerge. In short, ours is a time that will energize, disorient, and enrage. It will also change everything.

So how do we get through it? Do we merely survive? Or do we thrive and, in the process, help to bring a better, fairer world into existence? To answer these questions, I need to show that our crosscurrent is the dawning of a new day rather than the replay of an old movement.

Is This the New Age?

I've wrestled with the idea of cultural evolution for many years. When I've shared my thoughts about this subject with others, I've been surprised and fascinated by the frequent assumption that I must be talking about the New Age movement. For this reason, I considered opening this book

209

with a disclaimer, but eventually decided to save this misconception for discussion in the final chapter.

The New Age movement arose in the late 1960s, and exhibited early signs (both anomalies and *ahas*) that a major cultural transformation might be underway. Although its influence has declined since the vaunted 1987 Harmonic Convergence, New Age concepts still boast many adherents

Never well defined, the New Age in its early stages thrived on deep inquiry into the most important spiritual, political, social, and ecological issues of the time. It proclaimed the decline of irrelevant values and inaccurate assumptions about the universe as it celebrated the rise of a new value system. In many of its manifestations, the New Age recognized interdependence as the core principle of existence. It called for the deep engagement of ancient wisdom with modern science, psychology with spirituality, and East with West.

The best of the New Age does indeed resonate with sea change and the two-wave hypothesis. And many of the most important early indicators of our crossing were woven into its core concepts. But the movement soon became less a mature early stage of the twenty-first-century transformation than a cautionary tale.

The Aquarian Conspiracy

Long fascinated, as a student and later a journalist, with developments at the cutting edge of brain research, Marilyn Ferguson was the first to popularize the notion that a major values shift was underway. Her *The Aquarian Conspiracy: Personal and Social Transformation in the 1980s* offered a thoughtful pop journalistic account of what was going on. Ferguson herself was deeply fascinated by the new science that seemed to be such a key element of the emerging web, but she touched other bases as well, including psychology, spirituality, ecology, and politics. The book includes a survey of some two hundred prominent, self-identified "New

Agers"; when asked to name the major intellectual influence in their lives, the great majority listed Teilhard de Chardin.

Hailed by prominent thinkers from a variety of disciplines, the book was also sharply attacked by fundamentalist Christian groups as a harbinger of the coming of the Antichrist. Perhaps more tellingly, *Aquarian Conspiracy* avoided the superficial, do-it-yourself mysticism that came to characterize the New Age movement in its late '80s and early '90s heyday.

What Went Wrong?

Many chroniclers point to the arrival of New Age celebrity culture (particularly associated with actress Shirley MacLaine) as the beginning of the movement's decline. Some spoke of the vulgarization of the New Age, noting its overlay of narcissistic smugness and obsession with personal mystical or magical power. A shallow understanding of reincarnation and the Eastern teaching of karma came to distance later New Agers from the real struggles and suffering of real people. Perhaps the best-known maxim of the New Age, that "we create our own reality," did the same. The social energy of the movement went elsewhere.

The best of the New Age was bright indeed. It reawakened many to the reality of interdependent existence. It began as well to open real access to the healing and transformative powers of consciousness. It redirected our attention to the awesome responsibility of planetary stewardship and the waging of peace. It had some of us believing in magic again.

On the other hand, much of what emerged in New Age packaging coalesced gradually into a fundamentalism of the left. Self-aggrandizing gurus assuring the faithful they need only listen to their own inner voices watered down the original principles of the New Age. Weekend seminar quick fixes substituted for a long-term walk down the spiritual path.

CHAPTER 10

The New Age movement made extravagant predictions and promises that went largely unfulfilled. Does this suggest that the sea-change hypothesis will prove to be similarly flawed? No, and the proof that the new wave is more substantive than the New Age is found in emergent values.

EMERGENT VALUES

Chapter 5 laid out the major landmarks of a sea-change crossing, from *ahas* to eddies. Introducing the concept of emergents, I wrote, "As the transitional stage—the *crossing*—draws to a close, the newer wave gives rise to often-surprising new forms. *Emergents* are the unlooked-for self-organizing patterns that shape much of cultural and biological evolution. In the context of a changing culture, they can bring new ways of thinking, new structures, and new modes of activism. A new wave is embodied in the emergent patterns it generates."

Remember that emergent values haven't arrived yet. In some ways, they are predictable; in others, they're definitely not. That mixture of predictability with unpredictability is the way with self-organization, the signature pattern of increasingly complex open systems (like cultures). Understanding and recognizing the emergent new values and possibilities of the new wave are *the* sources of clarity and hope in a time of cultural sea change.

These values don't emerge randomly, even though their surfacing may be surprising. The ant colony that rebuilds after it is destroyed has enough flexibility to move to a higher level of (ant-colony) complexity whose precise internal structures cannot be predicted. But the ants will not build a beehive, a termite nest, or a wheel. The degree of unpredictability is constrained.

In the context of human cultural advance, we can predict the emergence of progressive new values in every key sector but not their precise shape. Sufficient indicators are already in place, for example, to argue

212

for the likely emergence of evolved human attitudes toward war and peace, injustice and justice, and ecological degradation and stewardship. We cannot predict the precise forms these new values will take. We can, however, persuasively argue that they will involve new levels of creative complexity, awareness of interdependence, and—most important— integration of the principle fields of human inquiry and endeavor. Of course, not every development will be evolutionary. The three bench- marks are critical, therefore, because they provide measures for identify- ing genuinely evolutionary change.

The later New Age movement's style of prophetic revelation is not based on analysis of present trends but on access to knowledge denied to ordinary people. In this regard, it has come to resemble the prophetic dimension of Christian fundamentalism. The key lies not in the scrutiny of elements of reality but in access to hidden sources.

To understand the emergent values of a twenty-first century sea change, let's return to the four sages we consulted earlier:

- Teilhard de Chardin would argue that we can count on a steady increase in cultural complexity and increasing consciousness. He already believed in the 1930s that the twentieth century would wit- ness converging global awareness.

- Ilya Prigogine demonstrated that systems that pass into chaotic periods are likely to emerge into higher orders of creative com- plexity. Reflecting on the period of the late twentieth century, he wrote, "We are at a very exciting moment in history, perhaps a turn- ing point."

- Stuart Kauffman is in awe of complexity. In fact, he defines "God" as the awesome creativity that we witness as emergent systems give rise to orderly realities that are far more that the sum of their parts. He looks to evolution rather than to a transcendent God as the source of higher ethical values and behaviors.

- Robert Wright explores intracultural and intercultural interdependence as a key to emerging complexity in the human world. In other words, Wright sees interdependent cooperation as providing an ideal environment for new values to emerge.

Together, our four voices suggest the benchmarks are reliable. The horizonal values that will continue to emerge during the next several years will urge our transitional culture toward greater creative complexity and an intensification of consciousness. The open system that is twenty-first-century culture will experience perturbations, and "bifurcation points" (see Prigogine in chapter 3) from which it can leap ahead to a higher order of internal complexity (always a good). Emergent systems will surprise but not disappoint us as we evolve ethically. And the interdependence of every system with every other will become not only more pronounced but also more apparent in our horizonal future. All in all, the report from the evolutionary front is hopeful indeed.

During the crossing, however, evolutionary surges produce emergent values. But there is also an opposing force of eddies, and the following section asks a question that anyone skeptical of the "things-are-getting-better" school might ask.

Where Do Eddies Go?

Will the whirlpools of antiscience, antifeminism, neoimperialism, and fundamentalism continue their destructive spin through the whole of the twenty-first century? Or do eddies tend to "unwind" over time? Is there, for example, a future for antiscience obscurantism on a large scale? It's certainly evident in the early twenty-first century, but how long can it endure? Several key dynamics very strongly suggest that as a sea change progresses, it dissipates the eddies of resistance. As the progressive wave gains amplitude, eddies slowly weaken and eventually fade away. Let's consider just three of the most persuasive of those dynamics.

Generational Metamorphosis

Considerable scholarly evidence and an abundance of anecdotal corroboration indicate that younger Europeans and Americans have become significantly more progressive over the past three decades. In other words, a generational value shift has occurred. Sociologist Ronald Inglehart has spent his long career studying the phenomenon of increasing postmaterialism in Europe and the U.S. He cites a strong correlation between economic advance and the turn toward progressive values, including self-expression, environmental protection, gender equity, etc. The highly regarded Inglehart-Welzel Cultural Map of the World suggests that as regions of the world move from industrial to postindustrial economies, their cultures tend to shift from survival orientation to self-expression.[1]

What about fundamentalism? Is it similarly subject to generational evolutionary influences? The so-called secularization model dominated sociological and anthropological explorations of religion for many decades. It maintains that cultural progress will diminish religious involvement. In other words, as societies advance, they will become more secular. Although secularization theory has been challenged in recent years, Inglehart, Pippa Norris, and others have recently offered strong confirmation of the correlation. They also found a significant tendency for "post-traditional" individuals to express an increased concern for the meaning of life; they became more interested in life's spiritual dimension.[2]

The next generation, particularly in the more developed countries, tends to be more worldly, educated, and globally connected. Moreover, the influence of European/American youth culture on young people in other cultures should not be overlooked. There are countless instances around the world (Iran in 2009 and 2010 comes to mind) of a greater values separation across generations than across international boundaries.

CHAPTER 10

The Rise of the Free Thinkers

Eddies tend to be strongly ideological, and ideology is in decline. People are increasingly aware that ideology represents closed systems of thought, preventing new data or new understanding from penetrating. As noted earlier, this is the "don't-bother-me-with-facts" position. In addition, ideological arguments have a tendency to oppose rather than to propose, and we're currently witnessing a strong sociopolitical reaction against "anti-this" and "anti-that." Ideologues are the intellectual equivalent of the identity-threatened individuals whose solution is to define themselves against others ("thank God I'm not a . . ."). As Aristotle suggested, an idea defined only in opposition to another idea is not fully formed.

The ideological cast of the "text" of most eddies embodies another weakness, illustrated by much of the literature of the anti-evolution movement. In general, neither the creationist nor the intelligent-design wing of the movement do original research. Instead, the many institutes at the forefront of the movement engage in mining the literature of evolutionists in search of problematic quotations or arguments that seem to contradict one another. No sustainable scientific enterprise can continue indefinitely in this fashion. It must inevitably become a caricature of real scholarship.

Finally, the emerging global youth culture renders ideological thinking still more vulnerable. The disconnect from the mainstream—a hallmark of the enclaves that embrace ideologies—will alienate all but the most securely sequestered members of the next generation.

The Information Storm

Information is the enemy of eddies. Searchable and sortable data about, well, almost everything, is now widely available. The desperate attempts of anxious parents, conservative politicians, and even totalitarian regimes to shut off the flow of volatile information testify to the fact that in the long run cyberworld wins. To be sure, the Internet is awash in pornography, hate speech, and drivel. But there are myriad ways to interact with the World Wide Web. One can graze, simply absorbing whatever one stumbles upon. Another option is browsing, a much more selective form of grazing, in which one accepts only certain forms of information or entertainment. Finally, one can be a hunter, knowing exactly what one wants to find and, in the case of the expert, exactly how to find it.

The rampant distortion that is easily deployed by counterevolutionary movements makes reasonably good use of the Web and is fairly successful in its manipulation of grazers. Eventually, however, the hunters must prevail. The search for valid knowledge has always worked that way. Learned and largely honest critics ridiculed Copernicus. In less than half a century, though, his views were being discussed in universities all over Europe. The real power of the hunter lies in the ability to discredit the deceptive arguments at the heart of an eddy. Terrorists or "freedom fighters" in the Muslim world, for example, have experienced a well-documented decline in support from the devout middle class that was for some time persuaded of their legitimacy. That fiction has become more difficult to maintain in a world in which the facts about terrorist activities are more accessible.

In the Web age, the enclave becomes extremely difficult to maintain, and sociocultural attitudes that require ignorance of the other begin to wither. The decline of racism and sexism in the twentieth century provides excellent examples of the ability of information to disarm bias that is easily maintained in isolation. Precisely because many eddies are phobic in nature, they can be dispersed by authentic encounters with the feared or hated other. The same is already proving true with pseudoscience. Gradually, the most extreme denials of biological evolution or anthropogenic global climate change become increasingly isolated; the more quickly and widely accurate information spreads, the less credible are these denials.

CHAPTER 10

Twelve Guiding Principles

Buddha gave the world the Noble Eightfold Path. It addressed three modes of existence: the cultivation of the inner life, the proper relation to others, and the understanding of important aspects of the real world.

The following principles for a time of crossing touch the same critical areas. Like the elements of the Eightfold Path and many other models for personal growth, these several areas of effort should be approached simultaneously rather than sequentially.

I hope that this brief section will serve several functions. It provides a useful general summary of the key ideas in the book. It serves as a brief compendium of inspirations and insights, a sort of *Handbook for Yeasayers*. Most important, however, is its role as a guide for cultural evolutionary explorers. It captures the essential vision of life in a time of almost unprecedented culture shift. It's not the first word about sea change, and I hope it won't be the last.

Figure 10.1. *Sea Change* (original art by Lonnie Hanzon)

Framing: A Preamble

Three thematic frames can help to envision an evolutionary lifestyle appropriate to an extraordinary time. The frames are just that: borders that set off an area for particular attention. The three I've identified should be familiar to you at this point: self, culture, and science. Reflection on the three frames is a discipline that generates clarity in thinking and prioritizing.

The first frame, Discernment, facilitates the examination of the interior/subjective aspect of the cultural journey. The second, Cultural Creativity, highlights potential areas for constructive engagement with other persons, groups, and communities in the evolutionary flow. The third, Walking in the World, directs our attention to the most important objective dimensions of the horizonal sea change. In more detail, they are:

- *Discernment*: Life decisions seem, at least in my own experience, to work out best when they proceed from a place and time of personal clarity. Most of the great spiritual traditions, for example, counsel their followers to engage regularly in a process of study, distillation, reflection, and contemplation/meditation. The initial aim is to maintain a relatively clear vision of oneself and the world one inhabits. Sometimes called *discernment*, the practice has application in a secular context as well. Discernment is the process of "getting to know me . . . all about me" and about the deeper levels of existence that are egoless but intensely real and sustaining. In the context of life in the crosscurrent, the process of discernment begins with critical questions: What is my strongest Yea? My cultural evolutionary center of gravity? The mode of knowing in which I'm most at ease? What are my greatest strengths, weaknesses, and openings for evolutionary growth? And what are the blessings I have to bestow?

- *Cultural Creativity*: As Paul Ray and Sherry Anderson have made clear, millions of "cultural creatives" are changing their own lives and enriching planetary society.[3] This frame thrives on interdependent engagement with individuals, groups, and cultures to improve and safeguard our world. Cultural creativity enriches social, political, and economic discourse and decision making. It is a powerful wellspring of evolutionary energy, and it creates the spaces in which I will encounter my *kalyanamitras* (see below).

- *Walking in the World*: Like a walk in the forest or along the seashore, our walk through the world finds immeasurable enrichment through right understanding of its rich, interdependent complexity. The true pioneer is eager to learn as much as possible about the scientific insights into the origin and evolutionary development of our universe, our planetary system, our world, and all the life it has ever hosted. Once one has begun to cultivate a real appreciation for scientific and systemic insights into the world we inhabit, walking in the world gives rise to a strong sense of opportunities for constructive engagement with a planet and a planetary community in transition.

The ongoing assessment of one's changing environment, interior capacities, and opportunities for action clarifies vision and generates hope. Moreover, the framing process combines the easily acquired discipline of examination with the more elusive skill of constant renewal of one's commitments. Most spiritual traditions, for example, teach that vows are not promises made for all time, but avowals, constantly renewed assessments of one's inner and outer realities, reappraisals of one's capacities, and *then* renewed commitment. Frames help to center that process in one's daily life. "How's my discernment coming along?"

As you proceed through the following twelve principles, consider each in terms of the three frames. What are its implications for my discernment, inner clarity, and centered self-aware life? What does it mean for the nurturing of my cultural creativity? And how can it shape my walking in the world?

1. Say Yea!

The quality of life in a time of sea change depends to some degree on whether we feel as though we're riding the old wave down and out or riding the new one in. While none of us is always in the yea frame of mind, we do need to cultivate the habit of saying yes to cultural evolution. At the same time, we should recognize our own internal naysayers and gentle them along. In short, we have to learn to live the renaissance as well as living in it.

Attend to the crossing and share the experience widely. Become a new storyteller. Communicate the stories of the waning and the rising. Become an adept in the application of the benchmarks of authentic cultural evolution. Remember that the real yeasayer is never the smug narcissist but always the apprentice and, at the same time, the journeyman.

In the Buddhist tradition, the bodhisattva is somewhat analogous to the holy wanderer found in other spiritual traditions. The bodhisattva seeks only the enlightenment of others, never his or her own. In that way, of course, enlightenment is secured. Similarly, the highest calling for the yeasayer is that of the catalyst, the one who works steadily for the cultural advance of people at every level of adaptive understanding.

2. Read and Interpret The Map

Real explorers often have a dual relationship with maps. Lewis and Clark had a very poor chart of the northwest portion of the American continent when they set off in 1804 on their journey to the Pacific Ocean. But they returned home with a much more accurate account of the route, its wonders, and its dangers. One of the most important preparations for voyagers in the sea-change crossing is a thorough acquaintance with the basic features of the passage: anomalies, *ahas*, evolutionary surges, eddies, emergents, and bygones. At the very least a rough map like this one is a must-have.

Moving beyond mastery of the map, develop the skills of crosscurrent cartography. In the years to come, we'll require better maps and journals of the first major period in human conscious evolution. Our own experiences along the way may seem inconsequential, but taken together in the creative cultural interaction they can help to shape the next generation's understanding of the crossing and its significance for humankind.

Recognizing and understanding the major anomalies of the older wave and the *ahas* that accompany the newer wave is essential. Bringing them to the attention of others is the next step. Appreciate the value elements of the older wave that are healthy and *not* anomalous. Perceiving the best values of the older wave in the good values of the newer is a critical skill; understanding how those older values may have matured into slightly altered forms is even more useful.

A good cartographer knows how to read a map's signs and symbols and their implications for the traveler. No doubt, eddies are going to appear on a number of paths. Familiarity with these eddies keeps other voyagers from their swirling undertows; such familiarity also offers comfort and courage by indentifying dismaying phenomena as only temporary manifestations of the crossing, and thus easier to endure.

3. Develop Spiral Intelligence

Spiral intelligence helps us know the stage from which we engage ourselves, others, and the world. At the same time, we need to be aware of the other levels at which we sometimes function. Identifying our spiral intelligence as centered, for example, on the green meme (communitarian, peace, justice, sustainability) with a strong grounding in orange (materialism, science, success) could open up a range of possibilities for self-reflection, refinement of understanding, and evolutionary advance.

For evolutionary voyagers, gradual cultivation of yellow (holistic, kaleidoscopic, evolutionary) is crucial; in fact, grasping all the cultural stages is important. This will help to eliminate destructive resentment of other stages. The cultivation of, say, a more generous communitarian activism makes each of us a much more effective evolutionary catalyst.

4. Know Your Quadratics

Once again we encounter the theme integrating the principle modes of knowing. The domains of knowledge and wisdom can be delineated in many ways; we can identify a number of interchangeable clusters of knowledge spheres:

- three estates (art, culture, science);

- three areas of inquiry (self, group, world);

- four quadrants (self, culture, science, systems science);

- four cells in a matrix (interior-individual, interior-collective, exterior-individual, exterior-collective); and

- four modalities (subjective, intersubjective, objective, or interobjective).

How we conceptualize the knowledge bases is important but not critical. Whichever formulation we choose, we must focus on two basic strategic questions: 1) How do we *see* the world? 2) How do we *save* the world?

The quadratic approach allows us to see the world in a broader, more insightful way. The cultivation of an increasingly "quadra-optic" habit of seeing ourselves and our environment is a surprisingly easy skill to begin to cultivate, and the rewards are substantial.

At the same time, we can understand situations and solve problems more effectively with a similar quadratic approach. Any question, issue, or object of study can be better understood through a multivantaged inquiry than from a single isolated perspective. I recently asked my son, a microbiologist, where the most exciting scientific research was taking place. His answer was immediate: "At the places where different disciplines are beginning to interact." We're not there yet; we're not using full quadratic inquiry regularly to bring the insights of self and culture together with those of science. The understanding that further integration is essential and unavoidable has, however, already become an emergent feature of the rising wave.

5. Embrace Complexity and Interdependence

Embrace rather than avoid complexity and interdependence. To do so means differentiating between increasing creative complexity and simple complication. That's the first step toward appreciating the link between increasing complexity and consciousness and the connection between complexity and the self-organizing emergent systems that lie at the heart of cultural evolution. Recognizing and relishing genuine creative complexity is a requisite crossing skill, one of the most important for life in the crossing. We develop it by employing a four-quadrant approach to every problem and engaging important issues from as many perspectives as possible.

Finally, we should note that interdependence is complexity's constant intellectual partner. The new interdisciplinary understanding means looking at the whole rather than individual parts. Once attention has shifted from parts to wholes, powerful new questions must be posed about the interdependent character of everything that constitutes those wholes.

6. Enculture Peace

Elise Boulding, the great Quaker peace activist, used to say, "Peace cultures thrive on and are nourished by visions of how things might be, in a world where sharing and caring are part of the accepted lifeways for everyone."[4]

Cultures of peace are those that promote and protect diversity. In contrast to warrior cultures, those committed to peace choose mutualism over adversarialism. They practice the morality of nurturance rather than the morality of old social and behavioral codes.

Evolutionary thinkers committed to the cultivation of communities of peace stress its complex interdependence with justice and ecological sustainability. Remove any leg from the peace-justice-sustainability tripod, and the others can no longer support the weight of a society.

Theologian Walter Wink, as we've noted, offers an evocative "new story" flourish to the peace-culture paradigm. Human societies since prehistory, he argues, have most often lived by the myth of redemptive violence, the story, told in countless variants, of good overcoming evil. That victory, however, is always accomplished through violence. It's a story that dominates the literature and imagery of our own modern society, the tale of the villain who just needs killing. Now, however, Wink and many others see a new myth taking shape, already emergent in some ways, still horizonal in others. It's the myth of restorative justice, the powerful new story that recognizes the interrelated values of peace, justice, and sustainability and teaches the lesson that peace can often be secured by restoring the missing leg of the tripod.

7. Pursue Third-Generation Rights

Today, we can speak of three generations in the evolution of our understanding of human rights. The first generation sought and often secured individual civil and political rights. First-generation rights were foundational in the political experiment that created the United States. Over the next two hundred years, however, the country struggled to define and secure the rights of groups. Now freedom rather than liberty became the new watchword. This second generation was marked by four great struggles: for the human rights of women, blacks, workers, and the poor. Today, many of the bitterest political battles of our time pit liberty (individual rights) against freedom (group rights). And now a third generation of the long evolutionary journey has begun.

Third-generation rights (*solidarity* is the newest term) are those that might be extended to all people and all cultures. The focus is now on rights to the global commons, to advances in technology and health care, and to the same opportunities enjoyed by the developed nations. The third-generation conversation lies at the heart of relations between the wealthy North and the poor South of the planet.

8. Sustain Seven Generations

The concept of seven-generation sustainability asks that each generation of human beings live sustainability and work with a commitment to improving the lives of those who will live as far as seven generations in the future. The principle is based on the Great Law of the Iroquois nation: "In every deliberation, we must consider the impact on the seventh generation . . . even if it requires having skin as thick as the bark of a pine."

A major older-wave anomaly is its profound misunderstanding and mistreatment of the Earth. A strong newer-wave advance is the clear sense that long-term generational life on Earth is impossible without a harmonious relationship with the planet itself and with all life. Whether the present sea change succeeds or fails depends in no small measure on converting that desire into action. The successful navigator of the change will have a steadily deepening ecological awareness and commitment.

A strong influence on that awareness is already emergent in the deep-ecology movement, which advances the welfare of the nonhuman over that of the human world. In contrast to so-called shallow ecology committed to technological remedies that secure anthropocentric concerns, deep ecology calls for a continuously deepening inquiry, involving all four quadrants of knowing, into the appropriate relationship of humankind to the rest of the Earth community. Without question, evolutionary ecology is deepening. Bill McKibben succinctly frames the deep-ecology call for a cessation of human technological degradation of the Earth: "We need to do an unlikely thing: We need to survey the world we now inhabit and proclaim it good. Good enough."[5]

9. Facilitate Conscious Evolution

Not every individual or culture occupies the same evolutionary level. Yet every one participates in the evolutionary ascent. The greatest obligation borne by those who realize the powerful and precious character of our time is to assist the process of cultural evolution. The key lies in esteeming each evolutionary level's healthy manifestations and accepting that different people will be at different levels. The conscious evolutionist seeks to assist others to recognize their own anomalies, create their own *ahas*, and enter the next stage of the adventure. Evolutionists like Barbara Marx Hubbard and Brian Swimme stress the cocreative role of human beings in an evolving universe. They stress the full integration of the scientific, the cultural, and the spiritual in the shaping of humanity's future. Like Teilhard de Chardin, those who call us to full participation in conscious evolution share a compelling vision of collective awakening.

It's a heady prospect, but one that the committed evolutionary can hardly ignore. The bodhisattva's career begins with "the rising of the mind for enlightenment," a spiritual form of the realization that evolution of mind, spirit, *and* community is a fact. Once that experience has taken place, the bodhisattva strives toward the enlightenment of all.

Similarly, once one has really grasped the radical truth of accelerating cultural evolution, there's no turning back. It's one of those things you just can't unlearn.

10. Become a Global Citizen

Global citizens are cosmopolitans. Their world-centric outlook is a powerful antidote to the familiar variations of egocentrism: nationalism, racism, sexism, and intolerance in general. The true cosmopolitan is not a moral relativist but one who understands that plural truths are possible.

The global citizen is the cosmopolitan first and the patriot after. Understanding that true citizenship in one's own country or culture is not possible outside the context of full commitment to the planetary community, a globalist serves both. To be a true global citizen, aspire first to be a committed bioregionalist, knowing that we meet and know the world first by developing a deep knowledge of the place, the watershed, the community we inhabit. Being at home in our own bioregion makes possible a much richer appreciation of the way such regions interdepend in the global ecosystem and in the social structures of the global village.

Finally, the emerging global consensus of values is the text of global citizenship. The rising global consensus celebrates many things, including the self-empowerment of women, the needs of the world's children, and the fact that the global challenge is not just one of resources but of vision.

11. Celebrate Interspirituality

Growing out of over a half century of profound dialogue between spiritual and cultural traditions and practices, interspirituality acknowledges and explores the very different but convergent spiritual visions and practices that nourish all cultures. The late Wayne Teasdale, author of *The Mystic Heart*, coined the word "interspiritual." He expressed it as "the sharing of ultimate experiences across traditions." As he put it,

"Interspirituality is not about eliminating the world's rich diversity of religious expression. . . . Rather, it is an attempt to make available to everyone all the forms the spiritual journey assumes."[6]

Perhaps you're not a religious believer and have no interest in the existence of any transcendent reality. Not a problem, Wayne would say. You still have an inner life, and it can without question be broadened, deepened, and enriched. The exploration of interspirituality, as a matter of fact, sets aside the doctrinal disparities that separate the world's religious traditions. Buddhists do not accept the existence of a creator God. Jews, Christians, and Muslims do—though in appreciably different ways. But all can come together to share what their communities have learned about the deep inner workings of mind and the still deeper life of spirit. It's worth noting that humankind's earliest reflections on evolution were spiritual in nature.

12. Find Your *Kalyanamitras*

In Sanskrit, the sacred language of the Buddhist path, *kalyanamitra* means "good friend," but in that tradition, it has come to signify much more. *Kalyanamitras* are spiritual allies, companions on the evolutionary path, joined by a shared commitment to service to others. The companions provide the journey's vital inspiration and energy. The spiritual friend can't be sought out. He or she has a way of happening along when the time is right and the need is real. The trick is to recognize and to cherish that person. But more is involved than just finding our own spiritual partners; we are also to learn how to be one.

All sorts of relationships are possible, and each of them offers the possibility of personal and spiritual growth. But the relationship between *kalyanamitras* is unique. It is grounded in a shared affirmation that life is rich and good, that suffering can be transformative, that evolution is a reality, and that existence has a purpose. The real heart of the *kalyanamitra* relationship, though, lies in the mutual discovery by two or more seekers that compassion is more than just a word. Only in the intimacy of genuine partnership do we begin to discover that "feeling with" another being is not only possible, but also powerful.

Epilogue: Sea Change as the New Story

She is the heart of her community. As she sits on the hard earth of her desert home, her voluminous skirts spread about her, her spine straight and her head thrown back, she seems to the children who gather about her a sort of colorful mountain. And in a sense she is, the cosmic mountain, the *axis mundi*—the pillar about which the world revolves. The old woman is the tribal storyteller. She opens her mouth and begins once again to chant the ancient invocations that bless her retelling of the myth of creation, the story the children have come to hear. Hesitantly at first and then with growing confidence, the older children repeat the familiar words and then begin to share the telling with the grandmother.

A few years ago, when Bill Moyers invited millions of Americans to meet Joseph Campbell, the response was astonishing. A master of lore himself but also a scholar with a compelling story about the nature of stories, Campbell struck a particularly resonant chord in his listeners. The conversation about myth blossomed. The inquiry into the relevance of mythic themes for theology, psychology, spirituality, and personal growth took on a new energy. And the phenomenon still shows no real signs of abating.

The great stories, Campbell maintained, have at least four basic functions. 1) They orient us within our cosmos and disclose the mysteries of nature and of the times and spaces within which life unfolds. 2) They ground us in our social nexus, reminding us of the protocols, the limits, and the values that make our place and our time unique. 3) They aid us in the passages from one life stage to the next, recalling those first humans who walked the same path from birth into this world to birth into the next. 4) They arouse in us a sense of wonder, an awareness of the divinely mysterious character of all existence. Each of the dimensions of the sacred tales helps to shape, to support, and to guide the community; and the storytelling process itself is one of the richest expressions of the life of the group.

When we think about the role of myth and song and story in this way we can begin to understand what Thomas Berry meant when he suggested that the cultivation and sharing of stories about what matters most is the most sacred of the tasks of any community, and that our failure in this regard is intimately related to our modern dilemma. "It's all a question of story. We are in trouble just now because we do not have a good story. We are in-between stories. The Old Story, the account of how the world came to be and how we fit into it, is not functioning properly. We have not learned the New Story."[7]

When a community's relationship to its story becomes static, when the story no longer lives in retelling and embellishment at the hands of the storytellers and the children, its culture has begun to disintegrate. In a living oral tradition, there is no distinction between the old story and the new, since the telling itself is the process of renewal.

Lately, I think a lot about Tom Berry's challenge. That's why I find cultural evolution so empowering. It's a story that needs telling, and it's beginning to be told in a variety of powerful ways by committed and persuasive teachers around the world.

The new story is especially urgent in a time of sea change, one of the very rare periods of a potential evolutionary quantum leap. If the story of the evolution of human values over time is worth telling to the children around every campfire, how much more important is the story of an extraordinary time of crossing? And who needs to hear it more than those who are trying to thrive in a crosscurrent they may not understand?

Notes

Introduction

1. Thich Nhat Hanh, *Creating True Peace: Ending Violence in Yourself, Your Family, Your Community, and the World* (New York: Simon and Schuster, 2003), 60.

2. Jim Kenney, "Introduction," in *Cosmic Beginnings and Human Ends: Where Science and Religion Meet*, ed. Clifford N. Matthews and Roy Abraham Varghese (Chicago: Open Court, 1995), 6.

Chapter One

Epigraph: Seamus Heaney, *The Cure at Troy* (Derry, N. Ireland: Field Day, 1990).

1. Michael Lerner, *The Left Hand of God* (New York: HarperCollins, 2006), 78.

2. Paul H. Ray and Sherry Ruth Anderson, *The Cultural Creatives* (New York: Three Rivers Press, 2001).

3. Thomas Frank, *What's the Matter With Kansas?* (New York: Macmillan, Metropolitan Books, 2004).

4. Jessica Stern, *Terror in the Name of God: Why Religious Militants Kill* (New York: Harper Collins, Ecco, 2003), 91.

5. Amin Maalouf, *In the Name of Identity: Violence and the Need to Belong* (New York: Arcade, 2001), 103.

Chapter Two

Epigraphs: Charles Dickens, *A Tale of Two Cities* (New York: Macmillan Co., 1922), 6. Charles Darwin, *On the Origin of Species by Means of Natural Selection* (New York: D. Appleton and Company, 1870), 424.

1. Stephen J. Gould, "The Pleasures of Pluralism," *New York Review of Books* 24, no. 11 (June 26, 1997).

Chapter Three

Epigraphs: Robert Wright, *NonZero: The Logic of Human Destiny* (New York: Pantheon, 2000), 208. Pierre Teilhard de Chardin, *The Phenomenon of Man* (New York: Harper Colophon, 1976), 224.

1. Teilhard de Chardin, *Phenomenon of Man*, 224.
2. Ibid.
3. Stuart Kauffman, *Reinventing the Sacred* (New York: Basic Books, Perseus, 2008), 273.
4. Wright, *NonZero*, 6.
5. Ibid., 5–6.
6. Ibid., 234.

Chapter Four

Epigraphs: Jared Diamond, "Location, Location, Location: The First Farmers," *Science* 278 (November 1997): 1243–44. Karl Jaspers, *The Origin and Goal of History*, trans. Michael Bullock (New Haven: Yale University Press, 1953), 1.

1. Jared Diamond, *Guns, Germs, and Steel* (New York: W.W. Norton & Company, 1997), 92.
2. Ewert Cousins, "Religions of the World: Teilhard and the Second Axial Turning," *Interreligious Insight* 4, no. 4 (October 2006): 11.
3. Karl Jaspers, *The Origin and Goal of History* 1, 2.
4. Ewert Cousins, "Religions of the World," 12.
5. John Donne, "An Anatomie of the World," in *The Works of John Donne* (Ware, Hartfordshire, UK: Wordsworth Editions, 1994), 177.
6. Jean Bodin, *Theatre of Universal Nature* (1596), cited in T.S. Kuhn, *The Copernican Revolution* (Cambridge: Harvard University Press, 1966), 190.
7. Galileo, in a letter to Castelli (1613), cited in Stillman Drake, *Discoveries and Opinions of Galileo* (New York: Doubleday, 1957).
8. A. R. Hall, *The Scientific Revolution 1500–1800* (Boston: Beacon Press, 1962), 171.

Chapter Five

Epigraphs: Italo Calvino, *Invisible Cities* (Orlando, FL: Harcourt, 1974), 135–36. Ken Wilber, *The Marriage of Sense and Soul* (New York: Random House, 1998), 44–49.

1. Galileo Galilei, "Letter to the Grand Duchess Christina," cited in Laura Fermi and Gilberto Bernardina, *Galileo and the Scientific Revolution* (New York: Basic Books, 1971), 72.
2. Ken Wilber, *Marriage of Sense and Soul*, 56.
3. "*Ekam sataha vipraha bahudha vadanti*," *Rig Veda*, 1.164.46.
4. Mark Twain, *More Tramps Abroad* (London: Chatto & Windus, 1897), 132.

Chapter Six

Epigraphs: Ronald Inglehart, "Globalization and Postmodern Values," *The Washington Quarterly*, 23.1 (2000), 228. Edmund J. Bourne, *Global Shift: How a New Worldview Is Transforming Humanity* (Oakland CA: New Harbinger, Noetic Books, 2008), 1.

1. Wayne Teasdale, in "Compilation of Interfaith Quotes," Association for Global New Thought, http://www.agnt.org/seasonForgiving/Interfaith%20Quotes.pdf.
2. Tom Hayden, *The Port Huron Statement: The Visionary Call of the 1960s Revolution* (New York: Avalon, Thunder's Mouth Press, 2005), 27.
3. Ed Rykiel, "Scientific Objectivity, Value Systems, and Policymaking," *BioScience*, 51, no. 6 (2001), 433.
4. Steven Johnson, *The Invention of Air* (London: Penguin Books, Riverhead Books, 2008), 41.

Chapter Seven

Epigraphs: Homer, *The Odyssey of Homer*, Harvard Classics 22, trans. S.H. Butcher & A. Lang (New York: P. F. Collier & Son, 1909), bk. 12. Edgar Allan Poe, "The Descent Into the Maelstrom," in *Great Tales and Poems of Edgar Allan Poe* (New York: Simon and Schuster, 2007), 231.

1. Karen Armstrong, *The Battle for God* (New York: Alfred A. Knopf, 2000), xi.
2. John Sperling, ed., *The Great Divide: Retro vs. Metro America* (Sausalito, CA: PoliPoint Press, 2004); Stanley B. Greenberg: *The Two Americas: Our Current Political Deadlock and How to Break It* (New York: St. Martin's Press, Thomas Dunne Books, 2004).
3. Amin Maalouf, *In the Name of Identity: Violence and the Need to Belong* (New York: Arcade Publishing, 2001), 103.
4. Jessica Stern, *Terror in the Name of God: Why Religious Militants Kill* (New York: Harper Collins, 2003).

5. Terry Eagleton, *Ideology: An Introduction* (London: Verso, 1996), 13.

6. Thomas Frank, *What's the Matter With Kansas?* (New York: Macmillan, Metropolitan Books, 2004).

7. Karen Armstrong, *The Battle for God*, xiii.

8. Fareed Zakaria, "The Rise of Illiberal Democracy," *Foreign Affairs* (November 1997).

Chapter Eight

Epigraphs: Lionel Trilling, *Freud and the Crisis of Our Culture* (Boston: Beacon Press,
. 1955), 37. Don Edward Beck, "The Never-Ending Upward Quest," Interview, *Enlightenment Next*, http://www.enlightennext.org/magazine/j22/beck. asp?page=2.

1. Based on the thought of the late psychologist Clare Graves, the "Spiral Dynamics" system was developed further by Don Edward Beck and Christopher C. Cowan. See their *Spiral Dynamics: Mastering Values, Leadership, and Change* (USA: Wiley, Blackwell Business, 1996). Many thinkers, including Ken Wilber, have drawn on the basic cultural evolutionary concepts of spiral dynamics.

2. Albert Einstein, *The Merging of Spirit and Science*, cited in Lincoln Barnett, *The Universe and Dr. Einstein*, 2nd rev. ed. (New York: Bantam, 1957), 108.

Chapter Nine

Epigraphs: Ewert Cousins, "Religions of the World: Teilhard and the Second Axial Turning," *Interreligious Insight* 4, no. 4, October 2006, 9. Karen Armstrong, "A New Axial Age," interview, *What Is Enlightenment*, http://www.enlightennext. org/magazine/j31/armstrong.asp?page=2.

1. Ewert Cousins, "Religions of the World: Teilhard and the Second Axial Turning." *Interreligious Insight* 4, no. 4, October 2006, 12.

2. Diana Eck, *A New Religious America: How a "Christian Country" Has Become the World's Most Religiously Diverse Nation* (San Francisco: HarperCollins, 2001).

3. Cf, for example, Martin Buber and Maurice S. Friedman, *Meetings: Autobiographical Fragments* (London: Routledge, 2002), 30–31.

4. Ewert Cousins, *Christ of the 21st Century* (New York: Continuum, 1998), 7–8.

5. René Jules Dubos, *A God Within* (New York: Scribner, 1972), 251.

6. Brian Swimme, *Swimme 1: The New Story* (part 1 of 10-part video series), http://www.youtube.com/watch?v=TRykk_0ovI0.

7. Leonard Swidler, "A Vision for the Third Millennium—The Age of Global Dialogue: Dialogue or Death!" *Journal for the Study of Religions and Ideologies* 1, no.1 (2002), 6.

8. "Introducing Feminenza—A New International Network for Women," *Topaz*, 4 (2002), http://www.templatenetwork.org/topaz/04/en/04.html.

9. Thomas Berry, *Evening Thoughts: Reflecting on Earth as Sacred Community*, ed. Mary Evelyn Tucker (San Francisco: Sierra Club Books, 2006), 1.

10. Alan Race, *Christians and Religious Pluralism: Patterns in the Christian Theology of Religions* (London: SCM Press, 1993).

Chapter Ten

Epigraphs: George Lakoff, "The Obama Code," *Blue Sky: New Ideas for the Obama Administration*, Berkeley Law Blog, UC Berkeley. http://ideas.berkeleylawblogs. org/tag/george-lakoff/. Mary Evelyn Tucker, "Can We Evolve Fast Enough?" video presentation, Global Oneness Project, http://www.globalonenessproject. org/videos/maryevelyntuckerclip9.

1. Ron Inglehart, "Inglehart-Welzel Cultural Map of the World," http://margaux.grandvinum.se/SebTest/wvs/articles/folder_published/article_base_54.

2. See, for example, Ron Inglehart and Pippa Norris, *Sacred and Secular: Religion and Politics Worldwide* (New York: Cambridge University Press, 2006), 4.

3. Paul H. Ray and Sherry Ruth Anderson, *The Cultural Creatives: How 50 Million People Are Changing the World* (New York: Three Rivers Press, 2001).

4. Elise Boulding, quoted, *Peaceful Societies*, http://www.peacefulsocieties.org/About.html.

5. Bill McKibben, *Enough: Staying Human in an Engineered Age* (New York: Macmillan, 2003), 109.

6. Wayne Teasdale, *The Mystic Heart: Discovering a Universal Spirituality in the World's Religions* (Novato, CA: New World Library, 2001), 26.

7. Thomas Berry, "The New Story," *The Dream of the Earth* (San Francisco: Sierra Club Books, 1988), 123.

Index

INDEX

INDEX

INDEX

INDEX

Parliament of the World's Religions, 128, 131, 139

patriarchy
decline of, 11, 14, 27, 42, 102, 128
women and, 13

peace
corporate culture and, 20
justice, sustainability connection, 124, 132–35, 225
in modernity, 13
in Second Axial Period/Age, 197, 201
Seekers and, 23
in twenty-first century, 6, 14, 126, 225

Phenomenon of Man, The (Teilhard de Chardin), 52

phenotype, 37

philosophy, 20–21

phrenology, 106

Pico della Mirandola, 95

P, J, S Connection, 132–35, 225. *See also* justice; peace; sustainability

Plato, 82

pluralism, 23, 25, 27, 197, 204, 205

Poe, Edgar Allan, 142, 143

political action committees, 31

politics, 108–9, 149–52

Pomos (Postmodernists), 18, 20–21, 25–26, 107–8, 183 fig. 8.1

Port Huron Statement, 115

post-denominationalism, 205

postmaterialism, 215

postmodern(ism), 20–21, 41, 46–47, 49–50, 107–8, 41 fig. 2.1

postpatriarchal, 69

postracial, 49

power, 31–33, 117, 166–67

Prigogine, Ilya, 59–62, 213

privateers, 30, 31

Protestant Reformation, 84, 100, 103, 157

pseudoscience, 106, 110, 217

psychical curvature, 60

Ptolemy, 85

Puerto Allegre, Brazil, 136–37

Pyramid, Great, 77

Pythagoras, 82

Race, Alan, 25, 204

racial inequity, 49

racialism/racialist, 39-40, 46, 48–50, 102, 161

racism, 11, 16, 39, 49, 217

randomness, 48–50

Rawls, John, 127

Ray, Paul, 24, 220

reactionaries, 29

Reagan, Ronald, 164

recycling, 128–29

Reinventing the Sacred (Kauffman), 64

relativism, 107, 205

religio-fascist, 161

religion
in Axial Period/Age, 78–84
civilizational, 78, 80–81
creationist movement and, 152–54
dissociation of, 103
exclusivism, 11, 41, 105, 159, 204–5
fundamentalism, 159–64

Jim Kenney has been recognized for decades as a leader in the global movement for intercultural understanding. Working to promote harmony and cooperative action among the world's religious communities, he had a major role in the two largest interreligious gatherings ever held, the 1993 and 1999 Parliaments of the World's Religions (Chicago and Cape Town). He was global director of the Parliament from 1995 to 2002; and, in 2002, he founded the Interreligious Engagement Project, helping global interreligious communities address critical planetary issues.

Kenney is the cofounder and executive director of Common Ground, an adult educational center offering a wide range of programs on the great cultural, religious, philosophical, and spiritual traditions and their implications for every dimension of human experience. He is also cofounder and coeditor of *Interreligious Insight: A Journal of Dialogue and Engagement* and, from 1988 to 2009, was consulting editor and a regular contributor to *Conscious Choice*, an alternative-living magazine based in Chicago.

For over thirty years, Jim has lectured widely on political, social, religious, and cultural issues. Over the past decade, his research and writing have focused on cultural evolution: how human societies adapt—sometimes dramatically—to a changing world. *Thriving in the Crosscurrent* is the pinnacle of that work.

Here's hoping we're in for a sea change of the kind Jim Kenney describes. It will take real shifts if we're to deal with the problems bearing down on us, climate change most of all. And those shifts will, as he says, have their roots in our understanding of who we are.

—Bill McKibben, educator, environmentalist, and author of
Deep Economy: The Wealth of Communities and the Durable Future